Teaching Discipline & Self-Respect

To my wife, Kirn Kaur,
and our children,
Karta Kaur, Dharam Bir Singh,
and Ananda,
who have given me the gift of living to my highest values

SiriNam S. Khalsa

Teaching Discipline & Self-Respect

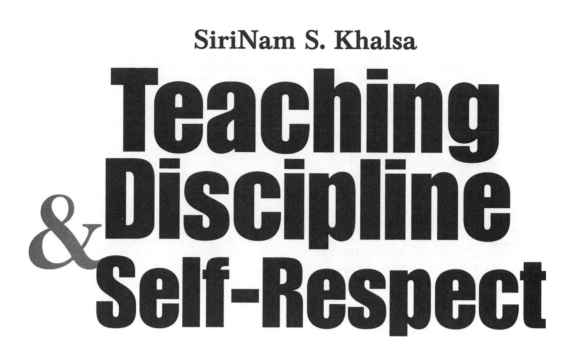

Effective Strategies, Anecdotes, and Lessons for Successful Classroom Management

Foreword by Jeffrey R. Ryan

CORWIN PRESS
A SAGE Publications Company
Thousand Oaks, CA 91320

Illustrations by Nathan Schiel.

For information:

Corwin Press
A Sage Publications Company
2455 Teller Road
Thousand Oaks, California 91320
www.corwinpress.com

Sage Publications Ltd.
1 Oliver's Yard
55 City Road
London EC1Y 1SP
United Kingdom

Sage Publications India Pvt. Ltd.
B-42, Panchsheel Enclave
Post Box 4109
New Delhi 110 017 India

Printed in the United States of America

Library of Congress Cataloging-in-Publication Data

Khalsa, SiriNam S., 1951-
Teaching discipline & self-respect: Effective strategies, anecdotes, and lessons for successful classroom management / SiriNam S. Khalsa.
    p. cm.
Includes bibliographical references and index.
ISBN-13: 978-1-4129-1547-2 (cloth)
ISBN-13: 978-1-4129-1548-9 (pbk.)
    1. Classroom management. 2. Self-esteem—Study and teaching. 3. Discipline.
I. Title. II. Title: Teaching discipline and self-respect.
LB3013.K55 2007
371.102′4—dc22

                                        2006031547

This book is printed on acid-free paper.

07   08   09   10   11   10 9 8 7   6   5   4   3   2   1

Acquisitions Editor:	Allyson P. Sharp
Editorial Assistant:	Nadia Kashper
Production Editor:	Melanie Birdsall
Copy Editor:	Susan Jarvis
Typesetter:	C&M Digitals (P) Ltd.
Proofreader:	Gail Fay
Indexer:	Michael Ferreira
Cover Designer:	Lisa Miller

Contents

Foreword

SiriNam S. Khalsa is a special education teacher in the inner city public schools of Springfield, Massachusetts, and his innovative, nurturing style of leading children to learning has garnered him a number of worthy accolades. I first met him when I was a judge in the competition for the 2004 State Teacher of the Year, and from the moment he entered the room, I was struck by how exciting and charismatic he was. He spoke of his students with earnestness, caring, and fervent passion, and I could tell immediately that his classroom must be a marvelous place for children to learn. It was vividly apparent that Mr. Khalsa is supremely dedicated to making sure that all of his pupils, no matter how troubled or initially difficult to manage, would be offered the chance to improve their skills, expand their knowledge, and improve their lives.

With the publication of *Teaching Discipline & Self-Respect: Effective Strategies, Anecdotes, and Lessons for Successful Classroom Management*, Khalsa has offered the teaching public a clear and lively manual in how to make discipline—often the bane of the educator's existence—a less overwhelming aspect of our job. While much has already been written on this subject, *Teaching Discipline & Self-Respect* is a concise and highly readable presentation of the essence of the issues. He emphasizes the vital importance of mutual respect between teacher and student and is an ardent champion of what I like to call democracy in the classroom. Some of our colleagues may wince at such a term, thinking it implies some pedagogical anarchy where teacher authority is crushed, students vote to determine grades, and where violent chaos reigns supreme. Khalsa and I would submit, however, that there is a vast array of behavior problems that can be neutralized by the transformation of the teacher-student relationship from a master-servant design to a much more collegial, cooperative partnership. *Teaching Discipline & Self-Respect* offers numerous ways of accomplishing this, from poignant anecdotes to specifically detailed outlines. In a time when much has been said and written about declining test scores and increasing dropout rates, Khalsa proposes ways to remedy these trends. He shows us how teachers can—with patient nurturance and unconditional respect—knock down the bastilles of student apathy. Khalsa gives inspiring advice on how to build barricades between our children and the pernicious forces of underachievement, crime, and drugs.

In these days filled with discourse about how educational paradise can be reached through high-stakes standardized tests, SiriNam Khalsa has offered solutions to our country's problem that are realistic, optimistic, and full of promise.

—*Jeffrey R. Ryan, PhD*
History Teacher
Reading Memorial High School
Reading, MA

Acknowledgments

My gratitude to all the difficult students I have ever taught (and will continue to teach). They have helped me to gain the skills necessary for teaching discipline. Earlier in my teaching career, I might have been a little unusual because I always wanted to teach students who were having difficulties with their learning and behavior. There were days when I would go home frustrated and upset, wondering how I could connect with and teach certain students who seemed to be beyond reach. There were also those days when I felt defeated because the students took over the classroom and little or no learning was accomplished. But I was determined to figure out how it was done, and fortunately realized that, just like learning in content areas, it isn't enough to simply tell students what you want them to know. I needed to teach behavior. My motivation to be successful with and empathetic toward those who were experiencing failure kept me focused on seeking ways in which I could have a positive impact on the students I taught.

Teaching a classroom full of difficult students is a gratifying experience nowadays. I am reminded of this every time I have an opportunity to coteach or to do demonstration teaching. The difference now is that, over a long period of time, I have acquired a set of effective skills and strategies. I was exposed to these skills through a variety of workshops and seminars, but most important as a result of having the opportunity to work with some very dedicated and talented people who possessed these skills. Some of these people taught children and others educated adults. During the time I spent with these people, I learned and absorbed valuable beliefs and lessons about how to relate to teaching discipline.

I am thankful to Dr. Joel Levine, school psychologist and author. Joel and I worked closely together for several years in a classroom that incorporated many of the cooperative learning and social skill strategies I now use and teach. Joel has a strong belief in the power of being respectful, empathetic, and professional with all students and parents. He helped me to acknowledge the importance of these values in my work with others.

Willette Johnson, former principal of John F. Kennedy Middle School and present administration coach in Springfield, Massachusetts, always supported me and continues to do so. She is a positive role model for administrators and educators who believe in the power of education, spirit, and perseverance. Mrs. Johnson also accompanied me when I was fortunate to receive teaching awards during our work together at John F. Kennedy Middle School.

I didn't learn how to teach discipline on my own, and did not think of all of these strategies on my own. My sincere thanks go to *all* of you—and you know who you are—who have contributed to my growth as an educator over the last twenty-five years. Thank you to all of my early inspirations, including Madeline Hunter and Jack Canfield, and all the coteachers and colleagues who shared my desire to learn how to reach and teach all children. They helped me to feel the freedom necessary to develop the skills offered in this book.

My spiritual teacher, Yogi Bhajan, who recently passed away, continues to be a "teacher of teachers." His guidance and clarity of purpose gave me inspiration and an understanding of how being a teacher looks, feels, and acts. I'm also thankful to my grandfather, Nunno Frank, who was my first mentor and who, in his loving way, advised me to become a teacher because it was a "noble profession." His advice was well taken.

Thank you, Nate Schiel, for sharing your special artistic talents and desire to support the quality of my book's presentation.

Thank you to Kathie Skinner, director of professional development, and all my fellow professional development associates at the Massachusetts Teaching Association for giving me the opportunity to share many of these teaching skills with other educators and paraeducators in our public schools.

I always admired the work Corwin Press did in offering quality books for professional educators. A final thanks to the staff at Corwin Press, and specifically Robert D. Clouse, editorial director; Allyson Sharp and Kylee Liegl, acquisitions editors; Nadia Kashper, editorial assistant; Melanie Birdsall, production editor; and the rest of the staff who were involved in supporting this book's production.

PUBLISHER'S ACKNOWLEDGMENTS

Corwin Press gratefully acknowledges the contributions of the following reviewers:

Michelle Barnea
Early Childhood
    Educational Consultant
Millburn, NJ

Cathern Wildey
Secondary Language
    Arts Teacher
Holiday, FL

Chuck Perkins
Consulting Teacher
    Explorer Academy
South Kitsap School District
Port Orchard, WA

Patrick Larkin
Principal
Peabody Veterans Memorial
    High School
Peabody, MA

Eileen Wascisin
Business Teacher
Lynden High School
Lynden, WA

Tammy Schoen
English Teacher
Coral Glades High School
Coral Springs, FL

Gwendolyn Quinn
Assistant Professor
University of South Florida
Tampa, FL

Kathie F. Nunley
Developer, Layered Curriculum™
    Method of Instruction and
    Founder, Brains.org
Brains.org and
    Help4teachers.com
Amherst, NH

About the Author

 **SiriNam S. Khalsa, MSEd, NBCT,** is a special education teacher, educational consultant, author, and National Board Certified Teacher. In his most recent position as Inclusion Coach, he supports the successful implementation of inclusive strategies in the middle and high schools of a large urban school district. He received a BS in Art Education and MSEd from the State University of New York at New Paltz. In addition to his work as Inclusion Coach with the Springfield, Massachusetts, public school system, he serves as a professional development consultant with the Massachusetts Teachers Association. He has received special recognition as 2002 Distinguished Teacher, as well as Massachusetts 1993 Special Education Teacher of the Year and most recently Massachusetts 2004 Teacher of the Year finalist.

SiriNam has been featured in educational articles, most recently the National Education Association magazine, *NEA Today* (January 2004). In addition to writing *Teaching Discipline & Self-Respect*, he has authored several other educational books, including *Differentiated Instruction: How to Reach and Teach All Students* (2004), *The Inclusive Classroom: A Practical Guide for Educators* (1999, 2005), *Group Exercises for Social Skills and Self-Esteem, Volumes 1 and 2* (1996, 1999), and most recently *Bullies in School: Interventions for Bullies and Victims* (2007). The strategies offered in his books are taken from over twenty-five years of experience teaching and learning from his students and colleagues.

SiriNam is married to Kirn Kaur Khalsa and is a proud father of three. He resides in Leverett, Massachusetts, with his family and can be reached by e-mail at sirinam1@rcn.com.

Introduction

About This Book

It is first-period Reading class, and you have prepared a dynamic lesson with an engaging activator and a purposeful summary. The overhead projector is all set up, and you have adapted and prepared curriculum materials for those students who have learning difficulties. After the first five minutes of the class, however, you realize that this lesson is sinking quickly. You decide to use a different approach toward engaging some students, but instead get into an argument over why they should spit out their gum. A student insists on tapping his pencil on the desk while another hides her head under her sweater. Before you know it, the period is almost over and little has been accomplished.

Sound familiar? I believe teaching is one of the most difficult professions of all because of one main factor: human behavior. Human behavior changes constantly. In the case of a student's daily life, changes are determined by myriad factors, such as what happened at home before school, on the bus, in the hallway, or entering the classroom. Consequently, the teacher who has prepared an engaging lesson can have his or her efforts thwarted due to a limited approach toward teaching discipline.

THE BOATMAN AND THE PASSENGER

Once there was a boatman whose job it was to ferry passengers across a lake. One day, as the boatman was about a fourth of the way across the lake, his passenger asked, "Have you read any of the great literature of our times?" To which the boatman replied, "No sir, I haven't." "One-third of your life has been wasted!" proclaimed the passenger. A few minutes later, the passenger asked the boatman,

"Have you read any of the great poets?" "No sir, I don't read that well," answered the boatman. "Two-thirds of your life has been wasted!" declared the passenger. At that moment, the boat hit a large rock and water began gushing in. The boatman shouted, "Sir, do you know how to swim?" "No I don't!" the passenger shouted back. The boatman said, "Well, your whole life has been wasted."

I tell this story when leading workshops to illustrate the importance of developing a variety of teaching skills and strategies because when a teacher feels like the lesson is sinking and he or she is losing control of the class, a large repertoire of skills is essential to stay afloat and regain momentum. *Teaching Discipline & Self-Respect: Strategies, Anecdotes, and Lessons for Effective Classroom Management* is all about learning effective skills and strategies that can keep you above water when you feel like you're about to sink. It's also about learning discipline strategies that guide students toward self-discipline and self-respect in a dignified manner for both the teacher and student.

It is not uncommon to hear from teachers that today's students are less respectful of authority and more difficult to handle. Many students have developed a negative attitude and genuine mistrust toward authority figures. Students' response to threats and punishments is usually, "So what?" or "I don't care." However, there is a positive outcome to this challenge of managing seemingly unmanageable behaviors. As with effective teaching strategies, educators have cultivated new approaches toward managing classroom behavior that *do* work with today's students.

Those of us who have chosen the honorable career of teaching understand that, in order to teach, we need to manage misbehavior in the classroom. We have also come to realize that some approaches are more effective than others. There are many books written on the subject of discipline and classroom management. Typically, books on discipline are created around a single system, such as the use of "behavior modification" or "logical consequences." At one point in my career as a professional educator—which I believe means a teacher who is constantly learning and growing—I came to understand the true nature of discipline, and consequently saw the inadequacies of a single system.

What is discipline? The word *discipline* has its roots in the word *disciple* and means "to teach or train." One definition is "to train by instruction or exercise." We are more likely to succeed in helping a student change their unacceptable behaviors when we use effective discipline procedures. It is part of continuous process of *teaching or educating*. As teachers, we understand that there is not just one method by which we educate our students; rather, we draw upon numerous strategies and approaches to reach and teach a very diverse population with a wide range of abilities and social/emotional needs.

There is no one approach that will work at all times with every student. There are occasions when all students respond to a discipline procedure in a congruent manner. But, generally speaking, the approach must be tailor-made to fit the age and personality of each student. In addition, some teachers feel more comfortable with one approach to discipline than they do with another. For these reasons, this book will offer a variety of strategies and approaches for teaching students desirable behavior (and how to avoid undesirable behavior). From these teaching strategies, you can select the ones that best suit your students' needs as well as your teaching style.

The strategies in this book put the focus on ways to assist all students to learn the most important life lesson: *self-discipline*. When we have sufficient self-discipline, many of our problems can often quickly be solved. Conversely, when we have little self-discipline, mole hills can quickly become mountains.

WHAT IS TEACHING DISCIPLINE AND SELF-RESPECT?

As previously mentioned, *Teaching Discipline & Self-Respect: Strategies, Anecdotes, and Lessons for Effective Classroom Management* does not take a "one strategy fits all" approach. Nor does it rely on punishment which comes solely from the teacher as an authority figure. It is an ongoing process of educating the student by achieving the following four basic goals:

1. Showing students what they've done wrong

2. Giving students ownership of the problem

3. Offering students ways to solve it and gain self-control

4. Leaving their dignity and self-esteem intact

An integral aspect of *Teaching Discipline & Self-Respect: Strategies, Anecdotes, and Lessons for Effective Classroom Management* is the use of prevention and intervention strategies that focus on developing an internalized sense of responsibility in students through alternative communication techniques and the use of realistic and palpable logical consequences. When we "discipline" children, we are actually assisting them to develop responsibility and *self-control*. It's easy for us to recognize the need for young children to establish self-control, but as children grow into adolescents they truly believe that they do not need controls or limits, and that without them they would do just fine. However, the fact is that, for both young children and teenagers, controls and limits do act as a source of *unacknowledged security* for them. This security is essential for managing a successful learning environment. When teaching discipline and self-respect, we also understand that the older the child becomes, the greater the developmental need for personal power. We understand that, in order to gain control, we must also give away some control through offering options and choices whenever possible. Unfortunately, some well-intentioned teachers take this theory to the extreme without following a guiding foundation based on sound beliefs and principles.

To further illustrate this point, imagine yourself sitting on a chair in the middle of a dark room. As you get up from your seat with your hands extended, looking for a solid object to hold on to, you touch a wall that quickly begins to crumble. How would you feel? What would you do? You would probably feel very insecure and most likely look for that chair and stay put. This image can be equated with the student who looks for limits and controls, but instead is given ambiguity and inconsistency, or a large dose of punishment which confuses and angers rather than educating.

Self-control can be equated with self-awareness, or being aware of the logical consequences of desirable and undesirable behaviors, then making the correct choices. We want all our students to learn valuable lessons about self-control and dignified social living.

OUTCOMES OF TEACHING DISCIPLINE AND SELF-RESPECT

A Feeling of Achievement

Teachers are able to fulfill their main responsibility, which is to help students actively engage in the learning process. A student who has changed a negative behavior cycle feels a sense of accomplishment and purpose.

Increased Professional Confidence

Every teacher is faced with the task of classroom management of problem behaviors. As we gain the confidence successful interventions bring, we can then more easily handle all our teaching tasks, including guiding the most disruptive students toward self-discipline.

Gaining a Healthy Perspective

Often our solution to misbehavior in the classroom is to react to the behavior personally rather than to approach the problem professionally.

This book's approach helps teachers to gain the needed perspective in order to be effective managers of behavior and consequently reduce classroom confrontations. As a result, we have a different mind-set toward what was once very disturbing. For example, a student acting disrespectfully now becomes one of the daily responsibilities of being an effective teacher, which includes effectively managing student behaviors.

Decrease Labeling and Increasing Change

Students who are prone to making poor decisions around how to act tend to be labeled "troublemakers" or "disruptive." When things get to this point, *labeling is disabling.* Consequently, we offer that student little chance of breaking out of a negative behavior cycle. The focus of teaching discipline and self-respect is educating both the teacher and student on the choices available, which can promote positive change and a healthy self-image.

Promoting Positive Feeling Tone

Creating positive feeling tone in the classroom promotes a genuine community of learners that can work cooperatively and support individual and group growth. *Teaching Discipline & Self-Respect: Strategies, Anecdotes, and Lessons for Effective Classroom Management* establishes a positive feeling tone by helping teachers understand how to develop better relationships with students, which in turn leads to improved cooperation. Educators who teach discipline agree that the goal of every school is getting students to cooperate, and that they get the best cooperation when they remember to provide many choices throughout the day. This book discusses the power of giving choices as well as guidelines to follow.

CHAPTER ORGANIZATION

Chapter 1 offers strategies and activities that assist a teacher in creating the foundation for a cooperative classroom, a foundation that supports task behavior and reduces undesirable actions. These strategies help students to feel more part of the classroom community, and therefore more willing to fully participate in the learning process.

Chapter 2 provides information and techniques on creating a positive classroom environment. This chapter also discusses effective techniques for reinforcing positive student behavior and attitudes.

Chapter 3 offers effective strategies for more direct teaching of discipline. Some are geared more toward elementary students, and others to middle and high school students. Most strategies are effective with students of all ages.

Chapter 4 addresses understanding and respecting students who are culturally and linguistically diverse. Teaching also requires an additional set of behaviors to address the problems and issues of students who are brought up in poverty— who make up an alarmingly high percentage of our students in urban school districts. A discussion of students with attention deficit hyperactivity disorder (ADHD) offers strategies to promote active support of and engagement with these students who have special needs.

Chapter 5 describes alternative interventions that can be used with students who are consistently disruptive and who act in unacceptable ways. I introduce these chapters with a method of objectively looking at a student's undesirable (and desirable) behaviors as cycles which tend to reinforce themselves. The next section offers a practical method for maintaining a professional approach to changing unacceptable behavior into acceptable behavior. To do this, we must first remember that the solution lies in discovering the purpose behind the misbehavior. Understanding the reason for any misbehavior unlocks the door to effective change. Conversely, identifying and supporting positive behavior cycles can be just as important, considering the nature of human behavior. This chapter would also be especially helpful to school counselors, behavior specialists, and administrators.

Chapter 6 describes eleven frequently reported undesirable behaviors that teachers are trying to manage every day in the classroom. Using "cycle diagrams" as a visual presentation for identifying each behavior cycle, I offer methods, procedures, and techniques to employ immediately for the purpose of changing the negative behavior as well as recommending mistakes to avoid.

Chapters 7 through 9 address the need for self-monitoring. Taking control of the classroom is often the most challenging aspect of teaching. Coupled with the many other facets for which teachers are responsible, controlling a classroom can create an abundance of stress in an educator's life. Consequently, I have dedicated this chapter to effective stress management for educators. We want to avoid walking down a road that can erode a teacher's initial idealism, resulting in burnout. I will offer common symptoms of being overly stressed, and present some of the strategies new and experienced teachers are using to regain their physical, mental, and emotional well-being.

Finally, I have included various lesson plans throughout the chapters for the purpose of promoting and teaching desirable behaviors. Activities and scenarios are sprinkled throughout the guide to interact with the information presented in the text.

1

Building Cooperation and a Community of Learners

The Heart of an Eagle Has Landed

THE HEART OF AN EAGLE

Once upon a time, while traveling from one place to another, a mother and her young son came upon a poultry farm. The boy was very curious and pressed his face into the wire fence to get a closer look at the hundreds of chickens pecking at the ground looking for food.

"Mama, there is a very odd chicken in this cage. He's not like the other ones at all. Do you see the one I'm talking about?"

As the mother looked at the bird her son was pointing to, a dusty man in dirty clothing walked up to them.

"What are you up to? I don't like people hanging around my chickens," he grumbled.

"Just looking, sir. But would you mind telling me about that bird in the corner there? He is an odd bird and in fact, I was thinking he might be a young eagle."

"Nonsense," the man replied. "I've had him since he was barely a hatchling. Listen boy, when something acts like a chicken and eats like a chicken, he is a chicken."

"Do you mind if we get a closer look for ourselves?" the boy asked.

"Do what you please," he answered.

The mother and her son bent in half to fit through the half-built door. She went on her knees and scooped up the young bird. "We think you're an eagle, not a chicken. You can fly free!"

She held the bird above her head and tossed him in the air. The bird flapped its wings once or twice but fell flat on its beak as it collapsed to the ground, and began to scratch in the dirt for its feed. The farmer, watching from afar, laughed out loud. "I told you that's a chicken, just an ordinary chicken. You're both wasting your time and mine!"

As the man turned his back on them to walk away, the boy shouted, "Excuse me, sir, but would you sell this bird to us? Since he's just an ordinary chicken, I'm sure you wouldn't miss him."

"Fine with me. Ten dollars is my price. Take it or leave it."

The mother knew the price was outrageous, but her son's eyes were pleading so she gave the old man the money.

The boy scooped the eagle to his chest, ran out of the cage, and began walking and talking to the bird. His words were words of faith that the bird would eventually know its true nature.

After the boy and his mother spent a few days with the bird, the boy suddenly ran down a dusty road. His mother followed him to the top of a small hill.

"What are you doing here, son?"

The boy did not answer. Instead he lifted the young bird as high as his arms would stretch and said as he had many times before, "You have the heart of an eagle. You are meant to fly and be free. Spread your wings and go, eagle, fly!"

A gentle current of air ruffled the feathers of the bird. The mother held her breath as her son tossed it high into the wind. The creature stretched out its wings and looked down on the mother and her son. He then began to glide smoothly in a wide circle high above the two of them, above the farm, above the valley.

The mother and her son never saw the eagle again. They never discovered where it decided to go. They only knew it would never return to live the life of a chicken ever again.

RAPPORT: THE POWER OF RELATIONSHIPS

A common mistake we often make as teachers is thinking one person can't make a difference. Like the mother and son in this African folk tale, told to me by another teacher and mentor many years ago, we as teachers need reminders to find the "eagles" inside our students. Many of our students who are caught in negative behavior cycles require support from one healthy adult to grow beyond their limited belief that they can't fly.

In order for this to happen, the effective teacher needs to fulfill his or her first responsibility of establishing an *emotional foundation* for all the teaching that will occur in a year. If we want to have an influence on helping students change undesirable behaviors, the first and most important step is to establish a good rapport with our students. By *rapport* I mean a synergy, mutual liking and respect between the teacher and the students. It can be characterized by trust, respect, and understanding. This rapport or positive connection formed within a relationship between student and teacher becomes the foundation for all interaction in the classroom. Rapport building can also provide important insights into the students' needs and interests.

OUTCOMES OF ESTABLISHING RAPPORT

Increased Sense of Security

Once trust and respect have been established within the teacher-student relationship, students are freed from the obstacles of worrying about their emotional, physical, and academic safety in the classroom. They can take comfort in knowing that, even in a crisis, the relationship they have with the teacher will be constant and continue to provide a safe environment in which to work through the crisis.

A Transformative Experience

Teachers need to be models for caring relationships. The teacher-student relationship can provide a context for personal growth in which students learn to care for themselves as well as for others. Students watch to see how their teacher responds to other students and teachers. They learn from the teacher's comments and make judgments about the intention behind the teacher's response. Is it to retaliate? Support understanding? Gain control? The model established by the student-teacher relationship can be used to develop new understandings about desirable personal interactions.

A Change in Responsibility

Building positive relationships can increase the trust that exists between teacher and student. As the teacher gives up the burden of being responsible for "controlling students," the outcome will be a more "manageable" classroom in which learning can occur. For this to occur, however, students need to be given more responsibility for their own behavior and learning, therefore relieving the teacher of the pressure of playing police officer.

HOW TO DEVELOP RAPPORT

I recently read that the three unwritten rules in real estate are "Location! Location! Location!" But how many teachers know the three equally important rules of classroom management? They are "Relationships! Relationships! Relationships!"

> It's evident that some teachers bring out the best in students, and some bring out the worst.

How can a student-teacher relationship be developed? One of my favorite middle school principals once made a surprising comment to me. She said, "Mr. Khalsa, I'm beginning to believe that there are some teachers who actually don't like children!" Instead, I choose to believe that many teachers struggle with the question of how to develop a positive relationship with their students. New teachers often hear from their well-intentioned colleagues, "Don't get to emotionally close to the students; you may get hurt and your authority will be undermined" or "If the students see you as a friend, you will not have their respect." I do agree that "being friends" with your students is not a desirable or effective goal; There is a myth in the teaching profession that states, "It is not important for students to like their teachers. However, they should respect them." However, in my many years of teaching in a variety of educational settings, I have always found that students work harder for some teachers than they do for others.

In effect, we teachers are salespersons, and common sense dictates that you can't sell something to someone if they don't like you or you anger them. Effective teachers have discovered along the way that a major part of their success is due to their ability to establish positive and meaningful relationships with their students. Teachers must therefore take the lead in developing such relationships. We need to demonstrate actively to students that we genuinely care about them, and to establish a healthy and *friendly* teacher-student relationship without trying to become a personal friend of each student.

It is also important to understand the psychology of students who are underachieving and/or who demonstrate negative behaviors in the classroom. These students have usually experienced years of a damaged self-concept. They see themselves as failures and as unlikable people. But my experience is that a student with such a poor self-concept is likely to make an effort to do school work for a teacher they really like.

Establishing a positive connection can be done in many ways; there is no one correct method. I've known teachers who come across as unfriendly and uncaring on the surface but whose names are always on the top of the list when students are asked which teachers they like most. Teachers have their own methods of establishing a caring rapport. Whatever method you use, the goal is to get across to your students that you genuinely like them, that you will enjoy teaching them, and that both of you will have a mutually rewarding time during the year you'll spend together.

I understand that not all students are "likable" and that some seem to go out of their way to be disliked. But, as one saying goes, "You have to remove a lot of dirt in order to find the gold." The gold is what we are looking for in our students, and with some it shines on the surface while with others it's hidden deeply under the ground. Regardless of their approach, if teachers do not take the time to get to know their students and establish a rapport with them as individuals, they will not be able to get these students to meet the challenges of learning.

For example, when I begin the year with a class of new students, I always concentrate during the first week primarily on rapport-building activities. I encourage the students to tell me a little about themselves, what they enjoy doing outside of school, their likes and dislikes, what pets they might have, whether they have brothers or sisters, what sports they like to watch and play, what they like best about school, what they hate about school, what music they enjoy, what they hope to get out of the year, and so forth. I also share appropriate information about myself as a teacher, a husband, and a father. This gives the students the feeling that I am genuinely interested in connecting with them as people. I know that, without rapport, they will not want to learn what I need to teach. Often bringing in a small photo album can start this essential process with students of any age.

Meaningful Dialogue

Meaningful dialogue with students is the key to starting to build caring relationships. Entering into meaningful dialogue in an open and honest manner can be done in several ways. First, it's important that the teacher be aware of any residual negative feelings or biases that might color the way they perceive the student. For example, if a student is frustrating the teacher because of his or her aggressive verbal comments, the teacher has a choice in how to look at the student. He or she can choose to see the student as a symptom or a behavior problem, or view the student as a person who has many facets to their personality, one of which is difficulty in controlling anger. By taking the second perspective, the teacher chooses to see the student as a whole person; this opens up new ways of interacting with the student that are not limited by one negative viewpoint. Dialogue with the student then becomes more genuine rather than superficial.

Two Scenarios

Let's look at two scenarios and the dialogue that ensued between the teacher and student which had two possible outcomes.

Mr. Worthy, a sixth-grade teacher, was asking his students to line up for lunch. Steven, who was near the end of the line, began talking to Sara and Jesus, who were standing in front of him. The three students were engrossed in their conversation when Jason, who was walking quickly to get in line, bumped into a desk that then hit Steven's leg. Steven immediately turned around and pushed the desk into Jason's legs. Mr. Worthy looked up just in time to see Steven pushing the desk.

Scenario One

Mr. Worthy feels the need to take a controlling stance. He immediately tells Steven to take his seat and explains that, because he cannot interact appropriately with his classmates, he'll have to eat lunch alone. He further explains to Steven that he will not be able to participate in the afterschool basketball game to which he has been looking forward all week.

Steven begins to protest and blames Jason for the incident. Mr. Worthy quickly interrupts him and explains what he saw, saying that if Steven continues to protest, a phone call will be made to his parents and he will need to be alone for the remainder of the school day. Mr. Worthy feels justified in his actions and thinks, as he's going to lunch with the rest of the class, "I have the safety of the class to think about. I can't let his behavior go unpunished."

As the class walks out the room, some of the students hear Steven saying, "You better watch out, Jason. You won't get away with this."

Scenario Two

Mr. Worthy has a philosophy about teaching discipline which revolves around the importance of students taking responsibility for their own actions and learning self-control. After seeing Steven push the desk into Jason, Mr. Worthy understands that Steven has lost his self-control. He immediately makes sure that Jason is okay and asks Steven to sit down and "cool off." After hearing Jason's explanation of what initiated the incident, Mr. Worthy asks the class to go to lunch with another teacher and tells Jason that if he wants to talk more about the incident, they can discuss it after lunch.

When the class leaves, Mr. Worthy sits with Steven and asks whether he is ready to talk about what happened. Steven, who feels safe with Mr. Worthy and trusts that his side of the story will be heard, nods his head.

Mr. Worthy begins by saying he is having a hard time knowing why Steven would push a desk into Jason. He then asks Steven to help him understand the situation.

Steven quickly says, "He pushed the desk into me on purpose! I know he did!" Mr. Worthy responds by saying, "Steven, you sound like you're still really angry."

Steven replies, "Yeah, that kid pisses me off just like his older brother. He's always doing stuff on the bus, and Jason just sits back and laughs."

"You felt like Jason was purposefully trying to bother you just like his brother does on the bus?"

"Yeah. If I let him get away with shoving desks into me, he'll never stop bothering me like his brother does!"

Mr. Worthy replies with understanding, "It's hard when older brothers pick on you. Sometimes it can make you feel helpless and scared."

"I'm not scared of that jerk."

"Do you think you get so mad sometimes that you act without thinking?"

"Yeah, I guess so. I've been told that before."

"You've been told that before?"

"My mother always says that to me."

"What usually happens when you act without thinking?"

"I usually get into trouble."

"Then how do you feel?"

"Not good. I know I shouldn't have pushed the desk into Jason, but I get so mad!"

Mr. Worthy then says, "Steven, I've noticed that you seem to be in what I call a negative behavior cycle. Do you want me to show you what I mean?"

Steven nods in affirmation. Mr. Worthy then takes out a piece of paper and draws three circles. He simply explains how the negative cycle begins with a self-image statement, like "I can't control my anger," and then moves on to a behavior which reinforces the negative self-image statement.

Mr. Worthy wants Steven to know that he understands his angry feelings and would like him to come up with ways to deal with them. He says, "Anger is a really hard emotion to control not only for kids but also for adults. Sometimes when we get angry we don't think clearly and do things we regret later. Would you like to work together on a plan to help you

Mr. Worthy's Negative Behavior Cycle

change your cycle into a more positive one, and therefore control your anger?"

Steven says, "Yeah. But what about Jason?"

Mr. Worthy asks whether he would like to try to work out his differences with Jason. He points out that they used to be friends at the beginning of the year and seemed to have a lot in common, like sports and comic books.

Steven replies, "Yeah, he has some cool comic books and we both are football fans. But it seems like he doesn't like me anymore."

"How about we all sit down together after lunch and try to work through this? It might not be easy but I think it's worth trying. What do you think?"

Steven agrees, "Okay, after lunch."

Mr. Worthy says, "Great, but until then I want you to stay away from each other. Let's go eat."

"Yeah, I'm getting hungry. Thanks, Mr. Worthy."

What's the Difference?

In the first scenario, Mr. Worthy did not enter into a dialogue with Steven, and therefore didn't understand his perceptions. Without dialogue, Steven had little chance of understanding *his* emotions or learning about the effects of his anger on his behavior. Learning how to control himself was not going to happen. Instead, Steven had strong feelings of vindication toward Jason. Children lose sight of their own responsibility when they are controlled by someone else—in this case, Mr. Worthy.

In the second scenario, Mr. Worthy entered into genuine dialogue with Steven. He did so without judgment, but with a desire to understand the situation and help Steven work through it in a positive manner. He could have controlled the dialogue and explained to Steven that it was an accident and that Jason deserved an apology. But he knew that Steven would probably become defensive and "turn off," and consequently would gain little understanding of his emotions continuing his negative cycle of reinforcing behaviors and attitude.

Mr. Worthy conveyed his understanding of Steven's perception and helped him to focus on his emotions without condoning his behavior. He also gained more information about what might be causing the animosity that had built up between these two students. He established a safe place for Steven to express his viewpoints. Then he drew on his knowledge about Steven, which was that Steven and Jason shared many interests and that their past relationship could be used to resolve this crisis. The incident was transformed through dialogue from a "punishable moment" to a "teachable moment" in which Steven was allowed to take responsibility for his own actions.

TECHNIQUES FOR CREATING DIALOGUE

Unexpected Questions

When I need to communicate with a student who has been misbehaving, I often dig into my "bag of tricks" for a technique that may open the student up to discussion and problem solving. One of my favorites when talking to a student out of class is asking a question such as, "I'm surprised you said what you did. Did I do something that bothered you?" There is always a good chance that, with a tough student, I may be able to avoid a power struggle by pursuing this line of action. If I'm treating the student with dignity and respect, the student is obligated to respond in a respectful manner by possibly saying, "No, Mr. Khalsa, you didn't say anything wrong." At that point, I may say, "OK, that's good to know. So what's bothering you?" Most of the time the student's response is genuine and mature, and they are willing to take responsibility for their misbehavior.

Active Listening and "I" Messages

A very wise teacher I once knew said, "If you want to support someone or 'stand-under' them, you must first understand them." The focus of active listening and the use of "I" messages is *understanding.* These techniques of communication were made popular by Thomas Gordon (1974).

Active listening is a way to communicate an attitude of empathetic understanding that does not necessarily require agreement with what's being said. There are several ways of using this technique when the student has a problem. You can use silent gestures such as nodding your head and sounds such as "Mm-hmm" to let the student know you're listening. You can also feed back or paraphrase what the student says at certain points in the dialogue. For example, Mr. Worthy used this technique when he said, "You felt like Jason was purposefully trying to bother you just like his brother does on the bus." Once students see that the teacher understands their perceptions without being accusatory or judgmental, they begin to feel safe in exploring their emotions and actions in relation to the situation at hand. Problem solving can be addressed more easily when a student feels understood. Modeling the active listening technique gives students a wider range of effective communication choices when they are listening to their peers.

"I" messages are used when you want to express to a student the effects their behavior is having on you. For example, "When *I* get interrupted,

I get really annoyed, so please listen." "I" messages can raise the expectations that a student will listen to your concerns and do what you ask. There are three parts of an "I" message that should be included for maximum effectiveness:

1. Can you describe the behavior? "When I get interrupted . . ."

2. How does it make you feel? "I get really annoyed . . ."

3. What do you want changed? "So please listen when I'm speaking."

Gear shifting is when you switch into active listening after sending an "I" message. This strategy takes a certain amount of personal awareness and self-control to be effective. This aspect of Gordon's (1974) system is often overlooked and can be the most demanding part. For example, the teacher says, "Joey, I get annoyed when you make those faces during class. They are distracting to me as well as others. Can you control your urge to make those silly faces?" Joey says, "Yeah, I'll stop but Susan is a pain. She's always staring at me." The teacher responds with active listening, "You feel upset when Susan looks at you during class?"

No technique can be effective if it is not delivered with genuine passion and empathy. This technique is not used to teach the student the important lessons of life; it is intended to reestablish a relationship of understanding which will promote a change in future behavior. Effective teachers use the most effective techniques over and over again while still being aware of the other techniques available to them in their "bag of tricks."

Like all techniques in teaching, with practice "I" messages become more natural. Some of us may find using this technique of communication difficult because it doesn't fit our personality or because it means we have to make ourselves vulnerable. For example, a student might not really care how we feel, and may therefore reject the very premise of our caring intentions. I once overheard a very angry eighth grader respond to a teacher's "I" message with, "I don't give a sh** what you feel like. I'm leaving!"

One of the myths of "I" messages is that these statements are the only way to communicate your feelings to someone else. In fact, there are a lot of ways in which we can choose to communicate with others. I have found the key to successful communication is matching how and what you say to the person with whom you are communicating. Knowing the student's personality and the type of relationship you have developed will also determine how you choose to communicate.

I was once asked to help a twenty-year veteran teacher who was having difficulty with a new position in which he was placed. He was trained as a shop teacher, and because of district cuts in positions, he had been asked to be an inclusion teacher. This position involved coteaching. An opportunity for me to demonstrate how to coteach in a math class arose unexpectedly. However, while I was leading a dynamic activity with the math teacher, my veteran teacher was sitting at the back of the room reading a book. After the class, we sat together to discuss our observations. If I had used "I" messages with him, he would have thought I was indirect and maybe even wimpy. I knew that because I tried an "I" message with him once, and he laughed it off. During this conference, I used another technique I seldom use: I looked directly at him, and said, "Dammit, George, if you were my coteacher, and you were sitting in the back of the room reading a book while I was teaching, I'd ask you to find another teacher to work with! You get a paycheck like everyone else here, don't you?" The feedback I got from his coteacher after that conversation was encouraging. He said George had adopted a new attitude in the classroom and was more actively involved with all the students.

I have never spoke that way to anybody else I've worked with, but I needed that technique for George. The same attitude applies to students. Different students may need different forms of assertive communication in order to respond to your needs.

Another myth about using this form of communication is that if you use "I" messages, they will always work. While I have found that they often do work, this isn't the case with everyone at all times. As I explained, not all people will care about your feelings. However, "I" messages remain the best way I know to make a direct statement in a nonthreatening way.

The opposite of an "I" message is a "You" message. "I" messages often lead to understanding while "You" messages suggest blame and result in arguments, resentment, and retaliation. An example of a "You" message is, "You keep interrupting me! You are so rude and don't care about anyone but yourself. Stop interrupting me." Both students and teachers are individuals with needs to be respected and met. It is advisable to avoid the use of "You" messages because they create more tension and disrespect, therefore failing to educate and facilitate change within the student (see Lesson Box 1.1).

Creating a Higher Standard of Communication

After observing a colleague using "I" messages and active listening techniques while talking to a student about his inappropriate behavior, I asked whether she had always communicated with her students about their discipline problems in this way. "Not really," she laughed. "I've been trying to be more aware of how I talk by not putting the student on the defensive. So I guess this is a new way of talking to students. My teaching life used to be filled with angry students and very frustrating situations.

(Text continues on page 22)

Lesson Box 1.1 A Lesson for Teaching "I" and "You" Messages

Materials

"What Are 'I' and 'You' Messages?" (Activity Sheet 1.1)

Setting the Stage

Ask students to think of a time when someone really annoyed them. How did they communicate their feelings? How did the other person respond?

Objective

Students will

- Practice identifying "I" and "You" messages
- Role-play giving "I" messages

Purpose

- To increase effective communication/dialogue
- To manage and resolve conflicts

Background Information

- Students need an understanding of role-play
- It is important to understand the meaning of assertive and aggressive communication (assertive is being direct without blaming or hurting the other person's feelings).

Instructions

Explain to the students that in this lesson they will learn the difference between an aggressive and an assertive way of speaking. The two alternatives are called "You" messages and "I" messages.

(Continued)

Lesson Box 1.1 (Continued)

"You" messages tend to be aggressive. They attack and blame another person. The receiver of the "You" message usually feels judged and blamed, and wants to defend himself. The result of a "You" message is usually anger, defensiveness, and perhaps long-term damage to the relationship.

An "I" message communicates your concern without blaming or judging the other person. The receiver of an "I" message learns that he has done something the speaker doesn't like. With "I" messages, there is less likelihood that the relationship will be damaged.

The teacher writes the following on the chalkboard:

- I feel . . . (Say how you feel.)
- When you . . . (What did the person do?)
- Because . . . (What problem is it causing you?)

Explain that these are the elements of an "I" message. Once you feel comfortable using "I" messages, you don't necessarily need to follow this format.

Ask students to pair up with a partner. They will select five or six statements from the "What are 'I' and 'You' Messages?" activity sheet to work with, deciding which of them are "I" messages and which are "You" messages. Then they will try to change the "You" messages to "I" messages.

Volunteer pairs can role-play changing the "You" message to an "I" message.

Summary

After the activity, discuss the difficulties students might have experienced in using "I" messages rather than "You" messages. Which would be more effective? Why do they think "I" messages are a better way to communicate? List reasons on the chalkboard and review.

Activity Sheet 1.1   What Are "I" and "You" Messages?

"I" messages express what you feel, what made you feel that way, and what you'd like to happen. Here are some examples of "I" messages:

- I really get embarrassed when you call out my name. I'd appreciate it if you would not do that in the future.
- I need some time to think about this. I feel pressured to say something I might regret later. Let's talk later.
- I really don't like you going into my desk without asking. Will you not go in without asking me?

False "I" messages are statements that have "I" in them but contain blame, demands, or accusations. These are false "I" messages:

- I think you're a liar.
- I feel like taking your CDs and losing them.

"You" messages use blame and threats to express feelings. Here are some "You" messages:

- You are really lazy.
- Why can't you do your own work and stop asking me?

Directions

Read the statements below. Write an "I" next to the "I" messages and a "You" next to the "You" messages. Then change the "You" messages to "I" messages.

1. Why don't you stop being such a loudmouth? _____
2. I really don't like it when you say things like that about me. _____
3. I'm busy, so just go away. _____
4. I hate it when my mother goes into my room when I'm not home. _____
5. I wish you would share. You're so selfish sometimes. _____
6. When you called so late I was really mad because I need my sleep. _____
7. I think she's really a liar and that's why I'm not talking to her anymore. _____
8. You used my CD player and never returned it. It bothers me that I can't trust you. _____
9. Can you stop tapping your pen? I'm trying to work and I can't concentrate. _____
10. You keep interrupting me! You have no respect for what I say. Will you stop it? _____

(Text continued from page 18)

I used to escalate mole hills into mountains by using so-called 'straight talk.' Honesty is crucial, but what good is it if the student doesn't listen and turns their anger on to you? By holding myself to a higher standard of communicating, I've enjoyed my job much more and like the results I'm having in changing unacceptable behaviors."

"I used to get so emotionally involved," she continued, "while feeling in my gut that I wasn't getting my message through to the student. I like using 'I' messages when a kid needs to understand how his behavior is affecting me. They seem to pause and see me as a person with feelings instead of an angry authority figure lecturing them on what not to do. I also used to do most of the talking when they had a problem. Now I try to listen and ask a lot of questions."

I asked, "Why ask so many questions?" "Questions help students to do the thinking and come up with their own solutions. Isn't that what we're trying to teach them—to think and solve problems?" she said.

STRATEGIES FOR CREATING COOPERATION

Photo Share

This is a strategy that should start at the beginning of the school year, but could also be done at different times throughout the year. I ask students who want to share photos about their life outside of school to bring them in for this activity. I always keep a small photo album of pictures of my family, pets, house, and so forth, on my desk for them to look

Photo Share

through when they have free time (students love to see pictures of your children or other people you spend your life with). I'll never forget a comment one of my students made while looking through my photo album. She said, "Mr. Khalsa, I never knew you had children and a wife, too!" Helping your students see you as a person first will only enhance your ability to create positive relationships with them.

Guess Who?

I've used this activity successfully at all grade levels. Students are asked to write on an index card one thing that really bothers them or a pet peeve, together with the name of a close friend and a favorite food. These questions can change depending on the grade and maturity level of the class. Questions such as your favorite musical group, TV show, or hobby are also very popular. The teacher participates in this activity as well. The index cards are collected and the students are asked to raise their hands and try to identify the person who wrote the card based on the information read out loud by the teacher. After all the students who want to guess have done so, the author of the card stands up. The purpose

Guess Who?

of this activity is to help students see connections between them by identifying shared likes and dislikes; it also helps to increase group cooperation and cohesion. Use these types of "getting-to-know-you" activities regularly to help all students learn about each other.

Private Appointments

I have found this technique to be essential in creating dialogue with the many students I teach. All students are asked to set up an appointment with me for a private discussion about whatever each of us decides to talk about. It could be school related—which it is the majority of the time—or related to other concerns the teacher or student might have. I've also spent this time talking about a basketball game we both watched on TV, or the reason girls of Puerto Rican heritage have a very large party celebrating their fifteenth birthday (*quinceañera*). It might take a week or two to get around to all your appointments, but the time spent is well worth it. Why appointments? To make certain you connect with every student.

Relaxed Time

William Glasser (1998) suggests that getting along with your students takes a lot of effort, and the best way to begin to do so is to have fun learning together. Laughing and learning are the foundation of all successful long-term relationships. I fully agree with Glasser's insight into fun and laughter and their effects on relationship building, as well as their role in inspiring creativity and reducing stress in the classroom. But in saying this, I also think we can do a disservice to our students if the message they receive is that school and learning should *always* be fun. I believe there is a time for relaxed interactions and feeling the enjoyment that comes from playing games and joking in class. But for most students learning is work, and they should understand that work is not always fun. Learning should always be challenging, stimulating, and expansive, but because of the nature of growth, it will not always be fun.

Rapport building doesn't stop after the first day or week of school. There are many times during the year when I must find the time to sit or walk with students and discuss what might be happening behind their surface behaviors. We also talk about frustrations they may be having in other classes. I take opportunities to call home to let their parents know I'm interested in how they are doing after school as well. This information always gets back to the student with the implied message, "My teacher must really care about me." When you're spending time with your students—especially doing things other than academic work—you are still teaching desirable skills for personal relationships. You are building the rapport that makes you a likable person. Teachers have a lot of competition for students' attention: video games, peers, MTV, the Internet, just to name a few. But we can provide something that these stimuli cannot: warm, caring, strong, and reliable human relationships. Our relationships will always have a profound effect on our students' achievement and lives. The importance of building an emotional foundation through rapport with your students might be summed up in the words of the poet John Masefield: "The days that make us happy, make us wise."

BUILDING A COMMUNITY OF LEARNERS

It's been my experience that fewer discipline problems erupt when students see themselves as part of a cooperative classroom community which supports sharing and caring behaviors. Learning is an active process in thinking, analyzing, and evaluating information. Building a community of learners can be a challenging goal, but it is essential for students to feel a sense of belonging. A thinking sign that reinforces this goal can read:

We work best when we are

All for One and One for All

Consider pointing out the basketball teams that succeed because of individual athletes deciding to be less of a ball hog and more of a team player (e.g., Michael Jordan or Tim Duncan). Discussing a thinking sign which supports cooperation is one way to begin to create an environment that is safe and caring for all students. In a safe classroom, all students participate and feel that they belong. They know that their individual and cultural differences will be accepted and valued as much as the things they share in common. Teachers ideally find the balance of showing students that every individual counts and can learn with a commitment to the well-being of the whole classroom community.

Building Group Self-Esteem

How does building a sense of classroom community help students to feel better about working and learning? For this question to be fully understood and answered, we must first understand the impact a person's self-esteem has on their ability to learn. Self-esteem is our sense of self-worth.

It comes from all our thoughts, and from the experiences we have collected about ourselves through life: smart or slow; awkward or graceful; popular or unpopular. These impressions, evaluations, and experiences we have about ourselves add up to a positive feeling about our self-worth, or a negative feeling of inadequacy. The connection between self-esteem and one's ability to learn has been made with students of all ages; high self-esteem promotes learning. Self-esteem affects virtually every facet of a student's life. Students who feel good about themselves usually feel good about school and life. They are able to gain the self-discipline necessary to meet and solve the challenges and responsibilities of life with confidence.

One primary condition affecting how individuals feel about themselves is a sense of connection, or the feeling a student has when he or she can gain satisfaction from group associations that are personally significant. The child in elementary school will experience shifts in his or her connections from parents to teachers; adolescents experience dramatic changes in connections to family, friends, and the world around them—from play-oriented ties to the rehearsal of adult relationships.

If you can "step back" and view your students objectively, you will be able to evaluate whether they have a firm sense of connection to the classroom community, or whether they are experiencing problems in that area and need assistance. Observable conditions that make up a community of learners include

- Students who communicate easily and are able to listen to each other and understand others' viewpoints
- Students who talk positively about family, race, or ethnic group
- Students who have a certain ease around their teacher(s)
- Students who don't always need to be noticed or in the center of activities
- Students who are able to state their ideas or feelings directly and ask for help when necessary
- Students who are comfortable expressing appropriate affection, such as handshakes
- Students who are actively helping each other to reach the learning standards set by the teacher

Models for Behavior

In cooperative classrooms, all students feel comfortable expressing their thoughts, feelings, and concerns. An effective way to start building a safe learning environment is for the teacher to model how to share feelings and concerns with the class. This could be done in a group setting or on a one-to-one basis. Students seem more likely to risk stretching themselves intellectually and socially when they know the teacher is understanding and supportive of an open and respectful process of communication—for example, "I'd like to share my concern about how much time I've been spending on reminding Kara and Crystal to stop talking during silent reading time . . ." Here the teacher is demonstrating a willingness to discuss something openly that might be interrupting the learning process without putting down or attacking students. This discussion could be brief but to the point. The importance of being a role model for effective communication cannot be underestimated when building a classroom community of learners. Some students come to school without having sufficient role models. If this is the case, the teacher will need to make them available at school. In doing so, he or she will help the students to feel secure about order in their classroom lives. They will be able to determine right behavior from wrong. With effective models, students' values and beliefs will serve to consistently guide their behavior and goals. They will have a sense of purpose and direction, they will understand how to work in a group, and they will know how to meet standards of excellence.

When the teacher is assertive about expectations of how to become a "genuine community of learners," the probability of it occurring increases. For example, one of my coteachers, Ms. Manfredi, and myself decided to take a different approach toward setting classroom rules at the beginning of the year. We asked the students what they thought about having a classroom that had no rules. One student remarked, "Well, last year, by the end of the year Mr. J had over fourteen rules we had to follow! No rules would be great." After some discussion, we decided not to have rules, but instead a guiding principle for classroom behaviors (see box).

Our Principle:

*You can do whatever you want in this
cooperative classroom as long as it doesn't bother someone else.*

We also made a point of saying that the teachers are part of the cooperative classroom, and discussed some behaviors that might "bother someone else." This approach might not be right for all teachers, but it was effective in creating a foundation for cooperative planning by placing the responsibility on the students for thinking about what behaviors might be bothersome to their peers and teachers. It helped to develop emotional maturity as well as independent thinking skills.

Students want to feel that their teacher is concerned both with their academic achievement and social/emotional progress. It has been my experience that when students expect the class to work together in ways that are good for everyone, they will actively help to bring that about. But I've also learned that we cannot assume that students, regardless of their grade level, will know how to actively support a cooperative classroom community without direct instruction and feedback.

For example, during the third week of school, Mr. Cauldron made the following announcement (which could have easily been made on the first day of school) to change a negative pattern: "I'm not happy with how students are treating each other in this class. From now on I want students to work toward becoming a class that practices mutual respect and caring. I want us to speak up if anything is bothering us, and work together to help each other solve our problems in an appropriate manner so we can continue to work and learn together. If we work together as a cooperative community of learners, I'm sure all of you, as well as myself, will really enjoy coming to school everyday and being a student in this classroom. Is this something we all want to achieve?" The purpose of his talk was to establish a clear expectation of cooperative classroom behavior, as well as to inspire students to think about their behaviors, and how they might work against or toward creating a genuine community of learners.

I don't believe any teacher wants to consciously disconnect from students. Although there are everyday events in the classroom that can leave students thinking they are dumb, disliked, and troublemakers, getting to know individual students and taking time to have a meaningful dialogue with each of them builds a strong teacher-student connection. Helping students to get to know one another through activities like those suggested in this chapter builds classroom community. Taking the time to reach students so they not only respect you but look forward to seeing you every day establishes bonds that stretch beyond the school year. A teacher can affect a student's destiny. You can never tell where your influence stops.

Whatever you cast a light on will grow. Celebrate your students' unique talents and strengths by consciously selecting something you can celebrate publicly for each student. This communication is best when delivered in a natural manner that is not forced or contrived. For example, "Amanda, I just want to mention to the class how much I appreciate how helpful you are. For example, . . ."

Creating Classroom Procedures and Routines

CHANGING BEHAVIOR CYCLES

I once read a study of middle school–aged children that indicated that 3 to 4 percent of the students who were underachievers could be labeled as "lazy" and needed some firm consequences or reminders to motivate them. These students often were tagged "unmotivated." But what about the other 96 percent of the students who were underachieving or labeled behavior problems? Their issue was not one of motivation but of self-image and self-esteem. Behavior is greatly affected by self-image—or how one sees oneself—and self-esteem—or how one feels about that perception. Students tend to behave in class according to the way they see themselves and how they feel about who they are in relation to others. In turn, their behavior will usually validate the self-view they already hold. This creates cycles of "reinforcing attitudes and behaviors." Depending on the child's self-image, the cycles can be either negative or positive. Understanding the reasons for misbehaving, and catching students achieving the smallest success in their behaviors and attitudes, can often begin to change a negative cycle into a positive one.

For teachers to be successful in today's classrooms, we must have a different set of skills and expectations from those of our own teachers. We need to teach more than just academic skills for our students to be successful. We must help our students to become aware of how and why they behave the way they do. This requires dealing with students at an interpersonal level. I recommend that teachers have a "cycle diagram" for each student. This diagram can be used to illustrate how the student is presently behaving (and why that behavior is occurring), and the possible interventions needed to change or reinforce the cycle. The cycle diagrams can be shared with the student, parents, and any other specialist or teacher working with the student. A dialogue such as this can take place:

Teacher: *John, I want to show you something that may be of help to you. You seem to be having a lot of trouble with other students in the class. My feeling is that you've had this problem in the past as well. Is this true?*

Student: *Yeah. Kids always bother me. They don't know how to keep their mouths shut!*

Teacher: *So, you think it's always their fault?*

Student: *Well, I think I probably cause some of the problems, too.*

Teacher: *Well, that may be true. Let's look how this behavior continues to reinforce itself and affect the way you see and feel about yourself. The way you see yourself is called "self-image." The way you feel about yourself is called "self-esteem."*

At this point, the teacher will show John a cycle of reinforcing behaviors. The discussion will focus on how this cycle may have developed and the behaviors that perpetuate its ongoing nature. Seeing the cycle can add objectivity to an emotional issue that has followed this student for years. After the teacher feels that John has an understanding of the cycle of reinforcing behaviors and/or attitudes, he or she can move on to how the old cycle can be replaced by a more functional one that supports positive relationships with John's peers. Figure 2.1 provides an example of what a cycle can look like.

DISCIPLINE VERSUS PUNISHMENT

The terms *discipline* and *punishment* are often used synonymously. This is unfortunate, as equating these two terms can create several problems. Punishment is usually what we do *to* the student. Teaching discipline is what we do *with* students. In general, punishment has little to do with the behavior it seeks to change, as well as usually being much too strong a consequence for the behavior. For example, taking away a student's lunchtime activities for not adequately cleaning up after a class is disproportionate to

Chris thought of himself as the child who always caused trouble. He thought of a lot of ways that he could disrupt the class; after all, that was his distinction. He teased the girls, he hid other students' book bags, he poured plaster of Paris in the art room sink. Each of these mischievous acts and others like them brought Chris the desired result—he preserved his self-image as the "class troublemaker." Chris was so desperate for attention that he was also willing to receive the inevitable painful consequences. He acted in ways to confirm his negative self-image. This negative behavior cycle would likely continue for the rest of the school year unless someone could help change it.

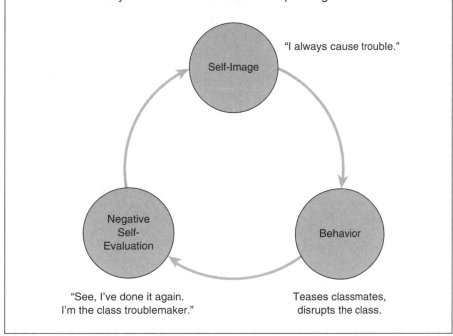

Figure 2.1 Reinforcing Behavior Cycle

SOURCE: Adapted with permission from S. Khalsa (2005). *The Inclusive Classroom.* Tucson, AZ: Good Year Books.

the severity of the act itself. Punishment tends to focus on what students are doing incorrectly instead of pointing out the positive alternatives available to them. In this example, the student may not have been told what "adequately cleaning up" entails.

The use of punishment is usually generalized to the extent that it can become self-defeating. Statements to a student such as "you're lazy" or "you're just trouble" focus on self-image instead of the learning to be accomplished. In fact, students who hear such comments over and over again usually resist learning as they think, "If I'm so lazy, why try?" Words that accompany punishment tend to lower the expectations of students and therefore create negative attitude cycles, which are supported by the negative behavior. We must be aware of the words we use with students, for they send an implicit expectation of how they should behave. The power of the words we use when "disciplining" is exemplified in the following story of "The Famous Baseball Player."

> A famous baseball player, who we'll call Sam Bass, won many awards while playing in the major leagues and retired as one of the best catchers in baseball history. After retirement, Sam Bass decided to become a motivational speaker. He would visits schools, universities, and prisons to try to inspire people to be the best they can be. While talking at a prison, Sam Bass told the inmates the story of when he was a young boy, and how he would play catch with his father every day after school. He shared the positive comments his father made, such as, "Sam you're going to be the best baseball player ever if you keep practicing." Then Sam would say to the audience, "And as my father said, here I am!" As he was walking out of the penitentiary after his talk, an inmate shouted out to him, "Mr. Bass, Mr. Bass, I also proved my father right!"

How many times have we overheard a teacher say while reprimanding a student words such as, "You keep this up and you'll fail this course" or "I'll see you again next year" or, in extreme situations, "You're headed for jail if you don't change." Expectations should not be taken lightly. Our students listen to our words and usually work hard at proving us right. Table 2.1 shows some of the differences between using discipline and punishment.

Educating is a process that enlists students to actively participate in their own learning. When we become angry, our natural instinct is to shut down and defend ourselves from more pain. Our entire personality often changes for the purpose of defending and protecting. Not unlike a cat whose hair sticks up and whose sharp teeth are backed by a troubling

Table 2.1   Differences Between Using Discipline and Punishment

Discipline	Punishment
Educates the student	Angers the student
Provides clear logical consequences	Enforces exaggerated and unrelated consequences
Focuses on prosocial behaviors	Focuses on misbehavior
Promotes self-discipline	Interferes with ability to learn

hissing, people tend to inflate themselves when angry and/or scared. Punishment often creates an angry reaction.

If the consequence fits the behavior, the student will make the connection and most likely remember the lesson in the future.

If the focus is on the misbehavior, the student will most likely want to repeat the behavior for dysfunctional reasons such as getting attention. If you do not want to have the misbehavior repeated, give the behavior little—or, when possible, no—attention. Placing the spotlight on what the student is doing correctly will give energy to that behavior and increase the probability of it being repeated.

> The goal of teaching discipline is to promote self-discipline.

Punishment creates attachments to external stimuli and cycles of negative reinforcing behaviors and attitudes. For students to stand back and gain a clear awareness or understanding of the consequences of their actions, they need to take ownership of their behavior and ultimately discipline themselves.

ALTERNATIVES TO PUNISHMENT

Teaching discipline, in contrast to dispensing punishment, promotes ordered learning. Ordered learning has guidance, direction, and purpose. Ordered learning is based on clear, logical consequences which lead to achievement and the development of self-worth (see Table 2.2).

Thinking of efficient logical consequences is not always easy and can take some planning. But the time is well spent because students learn better from what they tell themselves than from what we tell them. Using logical consequences takes the focus off the teacher—the outside authority—and puts it where it belongs, back on the student. Students

Table 2.2 Ordered Learning

Student Behavior	Logical Consequence	Illogical Consequence
Knocks over chair in anger	Picks up chair and arranges all chairs at lunchtime	Loses recess time
Walks in noisily	Walks in again	Receives detention
Shouts out teacher's name	Is asked to say it again but in a normal voice	Is ignored by teacher

may do what they are ordered to do, but their motivation to really change an undesirable behavior must come from their own inner voice. Logical consequences act as catalysts for thinking versus rebelling: "If I forget my textbook, Ms. Peal will not give me another book, and I'll just sit there feeling bored" or "If I walk into class making a lot of noise, Mr. Khalsa will just ask me to leave and walk in the right way." Students usually will respond better to a penalty when they see the logical connection between what they did wrong and what happens to them because of that behavior.

It might not always be possible to enforce a logical consequence in the classroom, particularly as quickly as you'd like, but any imposed consequences should always . . .

1. Be Enforceable

Being aware of not overreacting to an annoying behavior will help you avoid the "unenforceable consequence" trap. Ms. Bueti was so upset at her student's talking-out-of-turn behavior that she began giving a detention every time he blurted out an answer without being called on. By the end of class, she told me that the student had accumulated fourteen detentions! Then the student proceeded to tell her that he couldn't stay after school because his mother didn't have a car and he had to take care of his younger sister. Everyone was frustrated and the behavior that caused all of this was never really dealt with in a logical manner. It's often better to wait before giving a consequence than to quickly give an unenforceable one.

2. Fit the Behavior

Making the consequence logical or ensuring it fits the behavior may take some thinking or advice from a colleague or the student. Often the student can suggest ways to solve the problems they create if given an opportunity to do so. Maybe Ms. Bueti would have had more success if she included the student in the decision-making process. The following is an example of what this may look like.

Teacher: *José, it seems that you have a difficult time waiting to be called on before shouting out a comment or answer. What do you think might happen if you keep talking out of turn instead of waiting to be called on?*

Student: *I might have to sit by myself in Mr. Khalsa's classroom.*

Teacher: *Yes, that's a possibility. Anything else?*

Student: *I might get a bad grade for the day's work.*

Teacher: *You're right. That might also happen. Anything else?*

Student: *You might call my parents to come in.*

Teacher: *That's another option. Well, why don't we do this. If, as I'm teaching, I notice that you seem to still have trouble controlling your shouting, I'll pick one of those suggestions.*

It's been my experience that students will consciously try to control themselves after such a discussion. If, however, José doesn't change, I now have three "logical consequences" I can use for this particular student. The student has told me that leaving the class, receiving bad grades, and parental interventions have a connection to his behavior. For other students in the class, these consequences could be punishments and would increase resentment or another inappropriate behavior, which would expose the ineffectiveness of the consequence.

3. Be Administered With Professional Empathy

I was reviewing these guidelines with a high school math teacher who was having difficulty with classroom management. When I got to administering consequences with empathy, he gave me an awkward look and said, "You must be kidding." "Why do you say that?" I responded. He quickly said, "Look, when I've had to put up with some of the behaviors my students show me, I'm in no mood to be nice or feel bad for them!" I understood his frustration, but pointed out that whatever consequence he

> Empathy validates the student without condoning the negative behavior.

imparted would be diminished if combined with anger, sarcasm, or ridicule. A student who is receiving a consequence will usually reject the teacher's advice if it is paired with negative emotion. Using compassion and empathy when administering a consequence will create mutual trust and most likely have a lasting, positive result.

CLASSROOM PROCEDURES AND ROUTINES

At some point during my teaching career, I realized that a fundamental variable for successful classroom management lies in establishing and reinforcing classroom procedures and routines. By observing other teachers who seemed to have few problems with classroom management issues, it became clear to me that many discipline problems become very small or nonexistent when effective procedures and routines are established. A procedure is a classroom behavior you want the students to learn and a routine is the learned behavior occurring even without teacher supervision.

Most teachers do a good job of communicating classroom procedures at the beginning of the year. A sixth-grade teacher, for example, is very clear about classroom expectations. She tells her students, "To be successful in this class you must follow the four P's: Prompt, Polite, Participate, and Produce." This begins a dialogue of the four P's.

It seems the problems in effective classroom management occur when the procedures are not practiced and reinforced to the point that they become a routine. In becoming an effective teacher of discipline, one must also become an efficient coach for rehearsing classroom procedures. Classroom procedures and routines are reviewed frequently so that students understand the expectations for and consequences of their behaviors. Procedures include behaviors such as books and materials are in place; classes start on time; hands are raised when questions are asked; and students listen to the teacher and other students who are speaking. When a student is not following a classroom procedure, I will simply remind them by directly stating, "Raising your hand when wanting to speak is the classroom procedure."

Most students respond quickly when reminded in this manner. But when a procedure is not followed, the teacher's response is more important than the student's behavior. Before responding, think

- How can I make the behavior the student's problem?
- How can I offer a choice with reasonable limits?

During an assignment in which cooperative groups are working together, the noise level becomes increasingly louder until it reaches unacceptable levels. The stated procedure of not bothering others while working is not being followed. The procedure has not become a routine or a behavior which needs no reminding by the teacher. You see that an intervention is necessary for the class to return to a cooperative work-oriented environment. Students need feedback about their performance and assistance in returning to being responsible, not only for their learning but for the learning of their classmates and team members as well. Table 2.3 shows some options.

Students have an intrinsic need to know what the procedures are and how to perform them. When procedures are practiced and rules are followed, they feel secure in a predictable work environment. Being taught procedures is the first step. Using communication that supports student

Table 2.3   What Are Your Choices?

Ineffective Responses*	Effective Responses
"Be quiet!" "Do your own work!" "Don't you know how to talk?" "Okay, no talking for the rest of the class!"	"If everyone wants to continue working in groups, the noise level needs to come down immediately." "We can continue working in groups talking at a reasonable noise level or we could work individually without any discussion. What would you prefer?" "If I can hear Group Two from across the room, you're talking much too loudly."

*Some students might temporarily quiet down after one of these comments and others might take it as a personal insult and become defensive. Remember, your statements also reflect your values and beliefs around cooperation.

ownership of the problem and offering choices whenever possible will create a classroom environment that is both comfortable and motivating. When this is experienced, creativity and exploration can happen more freely. I discuss the importance of giving choices within limits in more detail in Chapter 3.

TEACHING CLASSROOM PROCEDURES AND ROUTINES

The Story of Multiple Personalities

One of my assistant principals shared this story with me. A new teacher was visiting our middle school and, after spending some time observing different classes and subject areas, she came to the conclusion that "these seventh graders have multiple personalities!" The assistant principal was interested in how she reached this conclusion. She assertively exclaimed, "Well, I observed one English class of seventh graders and they were working cooperatively, raising their hands, putting materials away without supervision and generally engaged in the learning process. I observed the same class in a Spanish class. What a difference! They were constantly interrupting the teacher and each other. Some were looking out the window while others had their heads on the desk. The teacher was always trying to get their attention while the noise level increased with every remark she made. My conclusion is that these students have multiple personalities."

Students Behaving

Students Misbehaving

The assistant principal shared his thoughts concerning her observations. He said, "Skillful teachers introduce rules and procedures on the first day of school. Rules are expectations of student behavior and clearly set limits for the student. Consequences reinforce the following of the class rules. Procedures are how things need to be done in the classroom setting, like how to enter the classroom, or put away materials, or even how to sit in your seat, but they also need to be taught and practiced. I see skillful teachers practicing classroom procedures all the time. These procedures turn into routines when the students show that they can independently follow the procedure without your constant intervention." He then went on to explain that what the visiting teacher had observed was one effective teacher in the English class who spent time establishing rules and teaching procedures, or managing the class. The Spanish teacher was sinking due to a lack of established rules, procedures, and routines. He thanked the visiting teacher for sharing her observations and set up a support conference with the Spanish teacher.

We use a variety of instructional strategies to help students engage in the learning process. Academic achievement and teaching self-discipline are approached in the same way. As in teaching academic material, helping students to understand how to stop working and listen for instructions does not always happen when the teacher only tells students what to do. We understand from pedagogical studies on how children learn that we cannot assume they always will behave the way we

> When we understand that discipline is not something we do to students, teaching will be much more satisfying.

want them to. Over a period of seven years, these seventh graders have been introduced to hundreds of rules and several teacher personalities. Ineffective teachers want to control students and/or catch them doing the wrong thing so they can "discipline" them. This mind-set is one created out of despair and confusion, and consequently results in temporary gain but permanent loss of change and control.

STEPS FOR TEACHING PROCEDURES AND ROUTINES

Step 1. Explain the Procedure

Always begin with a clear explanation of the classroom procedure. Next, model or demonstrate it. If the procedure has a few steps, demonstrate each one. For example, show how to walk into the classroom, sit down, and prepare for class instruction. I want to emphasize the "modeling" part of Step 1. Only about 20 percent of students learn aurally, or can be told to do something and understand it the first time. The other 80 percent learn either visually or kinesthetically. They need to *see* the behavior demonstrated, or practice it.

Step 2. Practice the Procedure

After explaining and demonstrating the procedure, it is important to practice the procedure—especially for the kinesthetic learners—until it becomes a routine. Having students practice the procedure will help them feel a greater sense of order and security, with an established expectation of behavior. If they do this under teacher supervision—also referred to as "guided practice"—it provides the best opportunity to do it correctly. The procedure becomes a routine when performed automatically without teacher guidance.

Step 3. Reteach and Reinforce

After practicing the procedure, determine whether all students have learned the procedure. If not, you may need to further explain, demonstrate, or practice the procedure. This process is called "reteaching." When the students demonstrate that they can perform the new procedure, reinforce the learning with praise or a privilege. Positive reinforcement increases the likelihood of that behavior reoccurring. When students "forget" the rules, it means they have not been reinforced for following the rules and procedures of the classroom.

When your students know, understand, and have demonstrated that they can follow the procedure, then it is their choice whether or not to follow it. Earlier, I discussed alternative strategies to punishment for students who choose not to follow a class rule or procedure. I will present many additional strategies in subsequent chapters.

Following is an example of how self-discipline— in this case, learning a class procedure—can be taught (see Lesson Box 2.1). An important part of this lesson is the process of using the three steps—explain, practice, and reinforce—to teach the procedure of how to enter a classroom and prepare for instruction.

Lesson Box 2.1   Entering the Class and Preparing for Instruction

Setting the Stage

Ask students why it is important to be able to walk into the classroom in an orderly way, and to know what the teacher is going to teach. Discuss what the class would be like if the students entered in any way they pleased.

Objectives

The students will be able to

1. Identify the reasons for entering the class in an orderly manner
2. Be prepared for teacher instruction
3. Rehearse procedure until practice is no longer necessary

Instructions

Explain to the students that you have a procedure for entering the classroom and preparing for teacher instruction. Demonstrate how you'd like the students to walk into the classroom; find their seats; take out their notebooks, text-books, and so on; and sit attentively, waiting for your instructions. Explain what you will do if someone fails to follow the correct procedure (leave class and enter the correct way).

Guided Practice

Practice by first asking a group of five or six students to demonstrate the correct procedure. Repeat this behavior rehearsal with small groups until everyone has rehearsed it successfully.

Independent Practice

Ask the entire class to practice the procedure. When all members of the class can perform the procedure independently, then praise the correct behavior and give positive encouragement throughout the week, month, and year.

   It is important to return to this lesson when the procedure stops becoming a classroom routine and the students need additional reinforcement.

THINKING SIGNS

The purpose of the thinking signs strategy (see Lesson Box 2.2) is to teach and remind a class of important truths about what creates a cooperative learning community, and to provide guidelines on becoming such a group. This strategy provides truths which liberate learning in the classroom and support individual as well as group responsibility. The teacher posts the easy-to-read thinking signs around the classroom or on a "Thinking Signs" bulletin board. The strategy is most effective when introduced at the beginning of the school year, but should be reviewed throughout the year.

Most classrooms have what I call "obedience signs" posted on the walls—for example, "Respect Everyone" or "Work Hard and You'll Learn" or "Change Tasks Quickly and Quietly." These signs tell students what to do. Thinking signs encourage students to reflect on the statements being made. They act as reminders of the essential elements of a cooperative classroom. One of my colleagues who teaches Algebra once pointed out to me that he wanted students to go home exhausted from all the thinking they did. His philosophy was that, whenever students think, they learn—and we can only offer them the opportunity to think and learn. This philosophy applies to teaching discipline as well. In Chapter 3, I address the strategy of using thinking words when problem solving with students. Lesson Box 2.2 presents a strategy for introducing thinking signs to a class.

FOLLOW-UP FEEDBACK

It would be easy if posting a sign eliminated students' anxiety about learning. We understand that many of our students resist participation due to the fear of not quickly understanding what is being taught. This resistance causes nonparticipation, which in turn can lead to a classroom disturbance, which then takes time and energy away from a cooperative learning environment. Thinking signs are most effective when treated as a first step toward reducing classroom tension and resistance toward active participation. The use of follow-up feedback is when the real learning occurs.

Grant Wiggins (Wiggins and McTighe, 1998) of the Center on Learning, Assessment, and School Structure (CLASS) reminds teachers that students do not learn without feedback. Praise is important in that it helps your students continue doing what you want them to do. The use of feedback offers students information for positive change. Follow-up feedback is value-neutral and only describes what the student did and did not

Lesson Box 2.2   Introducing and Discussing Thinking Signs

Setting the Stage

Explain to the class that creating cooperation in the classroom takes individual as well as group responsibility. There are guidelines supporting cooperation in the classroom that students need to discuss and understand. These guidelines will be called "thinking signs."

Objectives

The students will be able to

1. Gain an understanding of classroom cooperation guidelines
2. Reflect and discuss the meanings of the thinking signs
3. Summarize what was learned from the lesson

Instructions

Point to one of the thinking signs and read it aloud: "Mistakes can help one learn." Next, ask the students to read the sign aloud together. Explain the importance of making mistakes and using them as opportunities for learning: "When we try most anything new the first, second, and sometimes third time, we are apt to make mistakes until we get it. Can anyone give me an example of making mistakes until you have learned from them?" Possible responses can include learning a math concept, sport, a child learning to walk, and so on.

   After having the students read the sign aloud again, remind the students that mistakes are not bad but in fact are necessary in order to learn.

Summarizer

After repeating this procedure with three or four other thinking signs, ask the students to write something they got out of this lesson by completing sentences that begin with "I learned...," "I will remember these signs because...," I'm feeling...," This lesson was important because..."

(Continued)

Lesson Box 2.2 (Continued)

I recommend posting no more than three or four thinking signs at any one time. They can be replaced with new ones throughout the year. When making a thinking sign, be sure to write it large enough so students can easily read it from the back of the classroom. Some suggestions for signs include

- You are not supposed to understand everything the first time around.
- Successful students work together and feel free to ask for help from one another.
- Effective effort and strategies are the ingredients for success.
- Everyone can learn.
- Life is too difficult if we don't help each other along the way.
- If we can't see the good in all, we can't see good at all.
- Fairness is not everyone being treated equally, but individuals given what they need to succeed.
- We learn in our own ways, and in our own time.
- "Silent" and "Listen" contain the same letters.

do. In relationship to the "thinking signs," it is used to reinforce the meaning and value of the statements.

The following dialogue is an example of follow-up feedback. The purpose of this feedback is to support the student's understanding and integration of the thinking sign statement so they can relax, reflect on their learning, and learn with confidence.

Day One

Ms. Johnson: *José, I notice that you've closed your book and stopped participating.*

José: *Yeah, I don't get this stuff. It's just too hard for me to understand.*

Ms. Johnson:	*Yes, I see you're frustrated, but is there a thinking sign that talks about the problem you're having with this new math concept?*
José:	*The one that says you're not supposed to understand everything the first time around.*
Ms. Johnson:	*You're right. But it seems that you're not sure whether that is true for this classroom.*
José:	*Well, I want to learn this stuff but I just get frustrated and . . .*
Ms. Johnson:	*Give up. That's not acceptable, José. I do not expect anyone to understand exponents the first, second, or maybe the third time I teach it. But if you stick with it, eventually you will get it. Do you believe me?*
José:	*I guess so.*
Ms. Johnson:	*But I do expect all of you to ask questions and not give up on learning. Can I have your cooperation with this, José?*
José:	*Okay, Ms. Johnson. What do you want me to do?*
Ms. Johnson:	*Let's start by understanding that this is difficult to understand and that's okay. Open your book and ask me some questions.*

Besides the immediate goal of helping José relax and participate in the learning process, the long-term objective for using follow-up feedback is to help him to reflect on the importance of not having to understand everything the first time around. At the end of the day, Ms. Johnson reflected on her discussion with José. She realized that it would have been beneficial to begin the lesson with a brief discussion of the thinking sign. If,Ms. Johnson had begun with this discussion, José—and possibly others—may not have become needlessly anxious about not understanding the math concept the first time around.

Day Two

Ms. Johnson:	*Before we continue with our math lesson, I want to remind all of you that I don't expect you to understand exponents right away. Why do you think I say that?*
José:	*Because this is hard stuff and some of us aren't good at math.*
Ms. Johnson:	*Well, you're right that this is difficult and math doesn't come easily to some of you. But even for those of you who seem to*

do well in math, do you think it's okay for you to not under-
stand this right away?

Sharon: *Yes, it's still difficult for us to learn right away. (The class*
agrees and the teacher continues.)

Ms. Johnson: *But I do expect everyone to ask questions and not give up.*
Now our lesson . . .

While the students are practicing some problems in the text, José
raises his hand.

Ms. Johnson: *Yes, José, do you have a question?*

José: *Well, sort of. What happens if I never understand how to do*
this. Do I fail math?

Ms. Johnson: *You're concerned about never getting it. I can assure you that*
if you stick with it, José—which might mean staying after
school for some extra help—you'll eventually get it. But it
will not be easy and you can't give up.

José: *Okay. I'm not sure when to multiply this.*

Ms. Johnson: *Good question. Well, remember if you . . .*

After answering José's question, Ms. Johnson gives him feedback on
how he didn't close his book, but instead tried his best to understand the
math lesson by asking good questions. This follow-up feedback will help
José to adjust his behavior so he can succeed at learning. Intermittent
praise is now beneficial "to keep José in the game." Ms. Johnson decides
to begin the next day by reminding the students, "You're not supposed to
understand everything the first time around." She also decides to reinforce another thinking sign statement which addresses cooperative work.

Day Three

Ms. Johnson: *We now know that you're not expected to understand every-*
thing the first time around. But, before we begin today's les-
son, I have a question to ask you. Why do you think it's a
good idea to ask a classmate for help if you're confused?

Tom: *You're not always available and we can't ask you all the time.*

Crystal: *I like asking my friends for help. I think we can learn more*
that way.

Ms. Johnson: *Good answers. Okay, for today's lesson. . . .*

Once the standard and expectations have been announced, the teacher can use them as points of reference throughout the year. For example:

- Saying "stupid" to someone is disrespectful, and does not follow the behavior standards of this classroom. What else could you possibly say that would express your feelings without being disrespectful? (The teacher then invites a brief dialogue to remind students that there are alternatives to breaking the standards and to deepen feelings of assurance and acceptance.)
- I notice these three groups are following our cooperation guidelines. They are listening to each other, keeping their voices down, and being helpful to those who are still having difficulty solving the math problem. Keep up the good work.
- I like how José is asking for help by waiting patiently while I get around to answering his question. I really appreciate it, as I know many of you do.

Showing approval when a student relates well to others is important. Highlight considerate behavior, making a special point of it when you see a student cooperating and being helpful to others or yourself. Also encourage your students to take credit for successful interactions with others. By doing this, they will develop the inner evaluation necessary for becoming emotionally mature and less dependent on teacher praise.

As I mentioned, giving feedback will change behavior and praise will maintain the momentum of what you'd like to happen. If a student needs to be given feedback, it should be provided in a manner that is not attacking or emotional. For example, "Steven, tapping on the desk is bothering me and therefore not a behavior expectation of our class. I'd like you to stop. Thank you." Students who become frustrated with their inability to comply with class procedures can often become angry and disruptive. Lesson Box 2.3 can help them develop effective anger management skills.

Praise can be showered upon a student like direct sunlight, but for many students such abundant commendation is too personal and causes them to shy away from its positive intent. To be effective, praise should be specific and given with brevity. For example, "Steven, thank you for letting me finish making my point without interrupting me" or "I really appreciate the way you helped arrange the desks." Communicating in this manner invites students to become part of the learning community, which involves making mistakes and experiencing successes. Active participation will lead to ownership of the classroom behavioral goals and expectations.

Communicating Praise

Lesson Box 2.3   Understanding Your Anger

Objectives

Students will

- Gain a greater understanding of the effects of anger
- Develop effective anger management skills

Materials

"Understanding Your Anger" (Activity Sheet 2.1), chalkboard

Instructions

1. Write these quotes on the board and read them to the class:
   a. "Anybody can become angry—that is easy—but to be angry with the right person, and to the right degree, and at the right time, and for the right purpose, and in the right way—that is not easy to do." (Aristotle, Ancient Greek Philosopher)
   b. "The key to succeeding is learning how to control and use your anger for the purpose of achieving your goals." (Michael Jordan, six-time NBA Champion)

2. Discuss the different aspects of Aristotle's statement.

3. Discuss the possible meanings of Michael Jordan's statement on controlling and using anger.

4. Pass out the "Understanding Your Anger" activity sheets. Ask students to sit in pairs and, after studying the diagrams, quiz each other on the six things that occur when someone gets angry. Check for understanding.

Group Discussion

- After participants read and quiz each other (5–10 minutes), ask for volunteers to explain the six stages of anger.
- Volunteers can role-play the different stages of anger by demonstrating each stage with body language, as well as enacting an argument that triggers the emotional reaction.
- Explain how some stages are unavoidable, such as the release of adrenalin and increased heartbeat. Students have a choice to change the reaction of fighting or avoiding. Discuss what options may be acceptable and which may be harmful.
- This activity works best with groups that have developed a certain degree of trust and cooperation. It can be adapted for a beginning group of students by eliminating the role-play activity and having a group discussion rather than students quizzing each other.

Activity Sheet 2.1   Understanding Your Anger

Directions

Learn about what happens to your body and mind when you become angry. Discuss the six stages of anger with a partner (see Figure 2.2), then quiz each other to see how well you've learned what happens to you when you're angry.

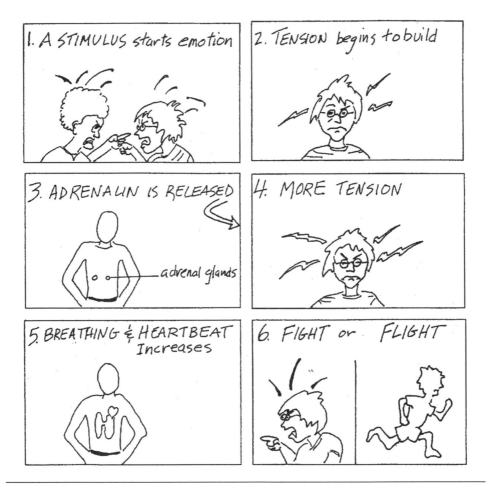

Figure 2.2   The Six Stages of Anger

Teaching Discipline and Self-Respect

WHO'S IN CHARGE? ESTABLISHING AUTHORITY

In order to establish authority in the classroom, we must first agree on what authority is. There are several definitions which can provide insight on how this term has been used and misused. Here are six different definitions of "authority":

1. *Reference.* Something that acts as a source for understanding

2. *Leader.* Someone who is a decision maker and pioneers change

3. *Influence.* Someone who can change the outcome of something through their clout or leverage

4. *Expert.* Someone who is a specialist in their profession

5. *Command.* Someone who rules through the use of control and power

6. *Teacher.* An instructor, coach, and guide who relies on mastery and wisdom

When I began teaching, I remember one of my instructors in graduate school telling me, "It's important to be an authority figure without being authoritarian." I don't remember his follow-up reasoning for that statement, but as I began teaching it started to ring true. In today's classrooms, students know that teachers (and families) simply don't have that "my-word-is-the-law-of-this-classroom" control because of the social, cultural, and technological changes that have occurred since the 1950s.

Students today know they have the civil right to be treated with respect and dignity, not autocratic control.

Now students—especially teenagers—say to themselves, "I'm not sure my teachers are right in what they are demanding of me. And my friends are saying that I don't have to put up with that because they can't make me do anything I don't want to do." No wonder new teachers are prone to early burnout and students are stressed from finding a way to survive with some of their teachers.

As teachers, we all hope that we can educate in such a way that, by the time our students are ready to move on to the next grade, we have seen observable mental and emotional growth. We assume that our adult friends will talk and act responsibly, accept limits, and understand when to be serious and when to have fun. So why can't we expect the same from our students? You're probably thinking, "You must be talking about someone else's classroom. My students have difficulty walking into the classroom without creating a problem. My authority means little or nothing to them."

But I am talking about *your* students and *all* students. The principles in this book are relevant to all classrooms at all age levels. If applied with consistency and awareness, they can assist you to take control of the classroom without losing your students in the process.

> Authority is a teacher who instructs, coaches, guides, and relies on mastery and wisdom.

We're going to look at the changing views of authority, and explore which definition can be most effective in making an impact on today's students.

I will present an alternative view on how to establish real authority in your classroom. Let's use the example of students being respectful in the class. Teachers have the right and responsibility to insist that their students treat everyone with courtesy and respect. So how do teachers exert their authority to reach this basic expectation of classroom behavior?

1. *Become a role model,* demonstrating through your behavior the expectations essential for classroom behavior. Teachers, too, must assess how they communicate with their students. It's hypocritical to criticize students for disrespectful talk or lack of courtesy while harshly commanding that they get their books out or using sarcasm as a means of discipline. This hypocritical behavior is one sure way to strip students' respect for a teacher's authority.

2. *Give orders only when it's absolutely necessary.* Giving orders only works when two basic situations exist. First, teachers or order-givers must be in unquestioned authority. It's not unusual for the assistant principal to walk into a classroom where the teacher is having difficulty exerting his or her authority and stating out loud, "The teacher is in charge. You do

not make the rules in this class." A few minutes after the administrator leaves, things revert back to their unmanaged state. Why? The armed services have to spend a lot of time training people to be good order-takers. However, some children and many teenaged students thrive on questioning authority, and the classroom is not the volunteer army.

Second, students or order-takers must accept that they would have a difficult time making a wise decision on their own in this situation. Once again, this is not difficult to establish in the military; however, as children become older, they tend to think they know everything.

So when should teachers give orders? When students are in potential danger or creating a situation that could quickly get out of hand, it is reasonable for a teacher to say, "Stop. You can't do that." When you do need to give an order, there is something else to consider. Once we give an order, it has to be followed "or else." This, unfortunately, is where I see too many teachers forfeit the little authority they may originally have had. The "or else" is very important. All eyes will be watching. It is also important to give orders only if you're able to apply meaningful consequences to disobedience. Remember, never give an order until you have first thought of a consequence for noncompliance, and then make sure you can follow up on the consequence.

Here are a few examples of orders given with consequences available to most teachers:

- "Don't throw pencils in class (or else I will take them away from you)."
- "Don't be disrespectful to me (or else I'll ask you to sit in Mr. Johnson's class)."

What are a teacher's alternatives to giving orders? Based on the premise that we want to keep our students in the classroom as much as possible, it is important to help students learn to make responsible decisions. Usually, teachers should be giving students covert messages that they will respect the teacher's ideas and thoughts but will be able to figure out answers for themselves. For example, instead of saying, "Pick up the mess you made" say, "Wow, there's a lot of paper and markers left on the table." When a student is sitting on a desk, instead of saying, "Get off the desk" say, "Desks are not for sitting on." These types of statements will promote internal versus external control, and consequently promote responsible behavior. Thoughtful teachers might also use phrases like these:

- "I would really like it if you would . . ."
- "I'm hoping that you could . . ."
- "I know you can . . ."

With this approach, you are modeling respectful behavior and giving the covert message that the student will comply with your request. Giving words of praise after a request is followed will naturally encourage future compliance.

Another alternative to issuing orders is to give a soft reprimand. Often this will be the only action that you will need to end misbehavior. Move close to the student, and address them in a friendly, but businesslike and firm manner. If possible, word the reprimand in a positive way. See Table 3.1 for an example.

Table 3.1 Hard Versus Soft Reprimands

Hard Reprimand	Soft Reprimand
"Both of you stop talking. Have some consideration for other students."	"This is quiet time. We need to be completely silent."

3. *Become an effective monitor,* moving around your classroom to check on students' progress. This is not a difficult task, but it will require effort before it becomes a habit. When you successfully monitor students' behavior, they feel you are in charge and in control of the classroom. Be sure to have the aisles clear of book bags so you can walk freely around the classroom without tripping. By paying careful attention to your students, you will help them to stay on task and consequently establish your natural authority. Further, any problems that may arise will stay small if you are actively teaching discipline through monitoring.

Monitoring from your desk is ineffective. Circulating among your students will keep them focused on learning. When monitoring, be aware of not spending too much time with some students and ignoring others. For example, don't spend so much time with one student (over two minutes) while the others wait.

Some teachers have established a signal system for monitoring their students' progress while keeping noise to a minimum. For example, teach students to give you a thumbs up if all is okay, and a thumbs down if they have a question. In the elementary grades, one idea is to tape three index cards together to form a triangle or tent that can stand on the desk. On each side you can place a signal for students to let you know how they are doing. A big question mark can indicate that they have a question, a smiley face would mean the student has no question, and a frowning face could mean help is needed.

4. *Act decisively,* giving students the clear message that you are not hesitant about the action you should take to manage inappropriate

behavior. Regardless of the approach you choose, you must exhibit confidence and resolve with your students. Students must see the teacher as strong enough to speak forthrightly, with no need to apologize for making responsible decisions. Acting decisively entails communicating assertive behavior, which is different from both aggressive and passive behavior. Being assertive means saying what is on your mind and standing up for what you believe to be right without blaming or attempting to put someone else down. What does decisive or assertive behavior look like? An assertive teacher communicates classroom expectations to students through clearly stated and carefully explained rules. Lee Canter (in Canter & Canter, 1976) calls this "assertive discipline," which is essentially a common-sense combination of limit setting and praise for following the rules. When observing a teacher exhibiting assertive behavior, you will see the following:

- The teacher stands in an erect posture, facing the student with whom he or she is speaking but maintaining enough distance so as not to appear aggressive or threatening.
- The teacher's tone of voice is clear and firm, but not so firm that it differs greatly from normal classroom speech. Any display of emotions in the voice needs to be avoided.
- The teacher does not speak and walk away or ignore the student's response, but rather listens to legitimate explanations while focusing on the message needing to be delivered.

Sometimes the most decisive action is to consciously choose to ignore misbehavior. This is effective if you first consider the reasons for the behavior and decide whether it can be tolerated. Use this strategy when the misbehavior is fleeting and if no other student is affected, such as in the case of daydreaming, chewing gum, or getting off to a slow start. Decisive action also may entail delaying the consequence for the purpose of helping the student and teacher come to a rational place in which a logical consequence to the behavior can be addressed.

The Case of Bin Laden

This story is an excerpt from an *NEA Today* (O'Neil, 2004) article in which I was one of the featured educators. It illustrates how the best decisive action was to delay taking action.

The slur came unexpectedly, shocking all who heard. "Bin Laden," the boy muttered under his breath as sixth-grade teacher SiriNam Khalsa passed his desk.

Testing Boundaries

It was nearly one year to the day after 9/11, and Khalsa, a striking Sikh with an uncut beard and turban, had just begun to sense the climate of respect he'd worked so hard for in his class at John F. Kennedy Middle School in Springfield, Massachusetts.

Now here came Louis with a curve ball. How to respond? An outburst, a public rebuke, a trip to the hall or the principal's office?

Khalsa, a genial man who coteaches the class, chose none of these. He knew a hasty decision would be unwise, knew also that every student in the class was casing his reaction. So he said calmly but firmly, "That kind of talk will not happen in this class-room. We are going to talk about it later."

Alone with Louis the next day, Khalsa asked, "What would cause you to say something so disrespectful and derogatory?"

"Well, you embarrassed me because you had called on me and I didn't know the answer," the boy replied.

Khalsa gently, methodically asked more questions. He patiently listened for clues. He made Louis know he was being heard. And by the time they were done, they had agreed to this pact: Whenever Khalsa planned to ask Louis a question, he'd first ask the entire class to think about it. "Then I'd walk by his desk and pause," Khalsa explains. "If he didn't know the answer, we agreed he could say, 'I need some time to think about it, Mr. Khalsa.'" (p. 24)

Dignity preserved. Respect modeled. A lesson learned for Louis and a whole class of adolescents testing boundaries of the adult world.

The approaches I offer for establishing authority are congruent with the definition I use for authority: a teacher, instructor, coach, and guide who relies on mastery and wisdom. This approach minimizes the opportunity for students to disrespect the teacher's role. But, as I have pointed out, if a student directly disobeys an order and the teacher doesn't thoughtfully apply consequences to the disobedience, students will lose respect for the teacher and his or her authority.

> It is often best to delay action when the action you would take could cause further disruption.

Establishing authority will help you to

- Keep students on task
- Avoid unnecessary power struggles
- Minimize problems
- Establish a classroom climate of thinkers and decision makers
- Maintain a respectful connection with every student and teacher

PROMOTING DESIRABLE BEHAVIOR

With a management system that focuses on prevention of problems, and a conscious effort by the teacher to promote desirable behaviors, generally most students' misbehavior can be controlled. Remember that this book is not a step-by-step foolproof manual; rather, it offers a wealth of positive teaching tools to help you form a belief system of how to control and enliven your classroom environment. Promoting desirable behavior requires consistent focus. It challenges you to take action with the heart of a lamb and the eye of an eagle. For example, many teachers have come to the realization that "catching students being good" is one of the most effective approaches in managing the classroom. All students like and want to be recognized. It is the teacher's choice to recognize their positive or negative behaviors.

> Catching students doing the right thing is based on the premise that the behavior that gets the most attention increases.

Skillful teachers spend time proactively looking for on-task behaviors to promote, creating a responsive classroom environment that prevents misbehavior from arising, rather than reactively dealing with problems after they arise. Promoting desirable behavior involves using positive incentives for students who are acting appropriately and making a conscious effort to catch them being good.

Unfortunately, studies have shown us that, for every positive comment in the classroom, there are four negative ones! That ratio, at the least, must be reversed. I once shared this study with my daughter who was in the tenth grade. She responded, "Papa, I haven't heard a positive comment from my science teacher in four days!" Sadly, this may be true in your school as well. Catching students doing the right thing has again and again been proven to be more effective in keeping students on task than the traditional lecturing and punishing of those who are off task. If you find it difficult to find positive behaviors to catch, the student is probably caught in a negative behavior cycle and may need direct modeling of the desired behavior. For example, "Jan, I want to show you how I'd like you to walk into the classroom and take out your notebook." Directly teaching classroom behaviors may become an ongoing lesson for some students. The message being given to the student is, "I will demonstrate how to act in this class because I have faith you will learn to act appropriately" versus "I'm going to catch you doing the wrong thing because you don't know how to change and therefore need to be disciplined."

Promoting desirable behavior is proactive. It includes the variables inherent in teacher-student communication, environmental considerations, and instructional adaptations. The following positive behavioral strategies offer effective suggestions for each variable.

Teacher-Student Communication

• Stand next to the door and greet the students individually as they enter the room, reminding them of the procedure for getting started (journal entries, math drill, checking homework).

• Prior to any activity, review behavioral expectations.

• Model behavioral expectations with guided practice and ongoing communication of the expectations to students and their parents.

• Catch students being good by giving attention to those who are engaged in appropriate behavior. Use social and verbal praise that is specifically describing the desired behavior, regardless of how minor it may be. "José is sitting still in his chair." "I like the way George is focused on reading all the questions." "Group Two is helping each other solve the problem." "Crystal has her assignment book out and open to today's date. She is organized and being responsible."

- Depending on the grade level, provide students with frequent activity breaks and opportunities to move around the classroom.

- Only give instruction when all students are listening and attentive.

- Be prepared to help those students who need support through transitions, change of activities, and unstructured situations.

- Circulate among the students by standing next to their desks, offering supportive comments, pats on the back, and so on.

- Increase the ratio of encouraging to negative comments to at least 4:1.

- Ignore minor inappropriate behavior; this can help to maintain the positive momentum of the class. It is important to train other students to ignore such behavior as well, and control their negative comments. When a student laughs at a classmate's attempt to be disruptive, I will respond by saying, "We don't laugh and therefore support another student's mistakes." This usually brings the class back to a neutral work environment without a long lecture or disruption.

- Offer alternative incentives for positive behavior (e.g., verbal praise; positive notes and calls to parents; certificates of achievement; earning time to do an alternative activity or tutor a younger child; extra music, art, or computer time).

Environmental Considerations

- Prevent the majority of classroom management problems through careful organization and long-term planning. Often a change in student seating and a move away from distracters will change an annoying behavior.

- Arrange desks so they have an ample amount of space between them if students are working individually.

- Have an assigned seating arrangement. It is helpful in preventing much of the disorder that can develop when students enter the classroom, which is the time that often sets the tone for the remainder of the period. And, most important, a seating plan can be crucial to contributing to a momentum. You know which students tend to sit together randomly throughout the room, with the resulting clumps of empty desks effectively diminishing the potential for that sense of cohesiveness and belonging that carries a class beyond the problems of management. Once the group feels that it is accomplishing something, it tends through its own momentum to control some of the counterproductive behavior caused by negative peer pressure.

• Use the strategy of flexible grouping to accommodate cooperative teams, pairs, learning partners, and learning centers. Often, giving very verbal students an opportunity to use "accountable talk" on your terms will increase their on-task behavior.

• Create a less stressful work environment by experimenting with playing calming music, turning down lights, or pulling down window shades. Reduce stimuli in the environment which may contribute to a students' difficulties.

• Have a designated place for book bags, coats, and any other objects that could interfere with easy access to all parts of the room and visibility of all students. Keep disruptive students close to you.

• Have a "print-reach environment," but one which is not so cluttered that students stop reading what's on the walls. Change the posters, student work, and so on at least once a month.

Instructional Adaptations

• Establish levels of expectations for accuracy and quality performance by using rubrics.

• Structure time units in order that students know exactly how long they have to work and when they need to be finished. Some teachers (in all grades) use a timer to keep students focused on the current activity.

• After giving verbal directions, point to a place on the board where they can be read.

• Give students from an individual written schedule of activities if they would benefit from knowing exactly what and how much there is to do in a day.

• Recognize accuracy and quality versus quantity and speed (e.g., display students' work, congratulate the students).

• Make sure lessons and activities are engaging and motivating, and that all students understand their relevance. Avoid excessive amounts of lecturing or "chalk and talk" instruction.

• Be careful not to assign seat work that a student is not capable of doing. This is an invitation to act out from frustration.

• Use effective questioning strategies. Too often a teacher will ask, "Does everyone understand?" or "Are there any questions?" and if no one responds they will move on. Many struggling learners will not ask questions out of fear that they may be seen as being stupid. Cooperative learning strategies such as Think-Pair-Share, Paired Heads, or asking for "thumbs up if you get it, thumbs down if you don't, and sideways if you're not sure," will help all students to participate in the learning process.

Think-Pair-Share is a strategy that provides students with time to think about a question, discuss it, and analyze it. The teacher asks a question or provides a problem needing to be answered. Students are then asked to first think about the answer without talking. After a minute or so, the students are asked to share their answer with a partner.

Paired Heads requires students to sit in groups of three or four. Each student is given a number from one to four. The teacher asks a question and the students in each group are asked to put their heads together to share the answer. The teacher then picks a number from one to four to select the student from each group who will share the answer with the class.

• Be sure to recognize struggling students when they indicate a need for help. Sometimes the best help to give a student with a learning disability is asking them to come up with a solution to their problem (e.g., how to find information in a textbook).

• Have clear options or choices of work for students who complete work early, in order to avoid problems that arise from "dead time."

PROMOTING DESIRABLE BEHAVIOR OUTSIDE THE CLASSROOM

Experience tells us that in many cases the most significant behavioral issues occur between classes—on the playground, during lunch, in the bathroom, and so on. Schools are dealing with these issues in a variety of ways. The following are recommended practices that have been found to be effective in promoting desirable behavior outside the classroom.

Elementary School

• Increase the amount of supervision to allow for adequate monitoring of students, especially on the playground and on the school bus.

• Teach students how to use playground equipment and enforce specific rules as to how supplies are checked out and returned, signals for lining up, and how to get in line without shoving or pushing in.

• Provide several choices of playground activities in which children can participate during recess. Having certain areas of the playground designated for particular games can be helpful. If you see that only one or two activities seem to dominate the playground (e.g., jump rope and tag), make sure a variety of games is available that can run with minimal supervision. Equipment should include things like rubber balls, basketballs, jump ropes, and hula hoops.

• Provide options for those students who don't feel safe or comfortable on the playground—perhaps having open library time or playing board or computer games.

• Assign trained student conflict mediators to help younger students who are observed to need this support. If they see a younger student (not their own peers) having difficulty handling a problem, they give them a choice: "Do you want me to help you with the problem or get a grown-up?" After completing a training course from the school counselor, conflict mediators have a very positive effect on promoting positive behavior.

• Missing recess due to a recurrence of misbehavior should be an option. All children want to be with others and to play during recess.

• Experiment with having students play first during lunch break, and eat after. Some schools have found that the children are calmer when they return to class after lunch. However, slow eaters can create another problem: not finishing eating before it is time to go back to class. Be aware of the possible consequences of your interventions. Some interventions may cause an unexpected "new" problem.

Middle and High School

• Our middle school came to the realization that most problems occur when there are too many students passing in the hallway between classes, going to lunch, and getting on the bus. A schedule that avoided sixth, seventh, and eighth graders congregating in the halls at the same time was implemented. Each grade was dismissed separately at the end of the day to get on their respective buses under teacher supervision.

• One middle school divided the eighth graders during lunch. All of the sixth graders ate with half of the eighth graders, while all of the seventh graders ate with the other half of the eighth graders. This intervention was found to be very beneficial for all students involved.

- Duty time for teachers was increased during passing periods.

- Bathrooms were kept locked, and could only be opened by a duty teacher. Bathrooms were also decorated by students with artwork and plants. This improved the cleanliness and reduced vandalism in the bathrooms.

- Parent volunteers were recruited to be at the doors of the school to greet students in the morning and to say goodbye at the end of the day.

INVITING COOPERATION

I originally thought that it was only during the first few years of teaching that teachers found getting cooperation from their students a challenge. I was wrong. In today's inclusive classrooms, where it is not uncommon to have students with ADD/ADHD (attention deficit hyperactivity disorder), students with learning disabilities (LD), and students with an emotional disorder (ED), both new and experienced teachers are having difficulty getting the class to just sit quietly and "cooperate." A major concern of all teachers is maximizing their instructional time. How can we do this without creating a climate which is uncomfortable and unmotivating? Understanding how to invite students to cooperate is an essential starting point.

> Cooperation is working together toward a common end or purpose.

Mr. Campbell, a middle school teacher, said, "I find that some students act as if their purpose is to stop me from teaching! I'd be in the middle of reviewing for a test when someone would ask for a pass to the bathroom, a student would get up and begin sharpening a pencil, and another would fall out of his chair. What is the matter with these kids? Don't they understand the importance of getting an education? Can't they make the connection between school and their own future? Why can't they try to cooperate with me so we can get some work done?"

Ms. Bontempo, an elementary grade teacher, was on recess duty as a group of students were pushing and shrieking at each other over whose turn it was to play with a ball. She rolled her eyes in disgust and said, "Look at all of them. Why do they continue to act so immature?" I thought, "Maybe it's because they are children, and that's how they sometimes behave." Even though it is normal for children to exhibit certain undesirable behaviors such as teasing, shoving, and complaining at different stages of development, often what we are seeing is more than just childish behavior. Some students are dealing with internal problems such as ADHD, which alter their ability to control their behavior. Others are dealing with external issues such as having little contact with their parents and consistent role models. Other students have one parent who can't be home because he or she is holding down a day job and a night job just to survive. An increasing number of students are also living in foster homes, and because of this are forced to move from school to school. Not only are these students coping with the normal problems inherent in growing up, but many of them haven't had a chance to be "children."

The effective teacher communicates to students in an adult voice. The adult voice invites students to cooperate without relying on demands, threats, lectures, or sarcasm. (See the scenarios below for examples of the use of the adult voice as it compares to the parent voice [typically authoritative and critical] and the child voice [naturally impulsive and emotional].) Skills that create cooperative behavior in the classroom have a foundation in the tone of your voice as well as in your words. The most skilled response can fall on deaf ears when delivered with a sigh of disgust that implies, "You've done it again. . . . When will you get your act together?" Along with words of respect, we need an attitude of respect that is reflected in our tone. This attitude sends the message, "I have full confidence in your ability and your judgment. Once I point out the problem, I know you'll know what to do."

I have found that these communication skills which invite cooperation in the classroom need to be practiced in order to be effective. However, changing old communication habits can be difficult when practiced in seclusion, so it is important to find a colleague with whom to share these skills and discuss their effectiveness.

SCENARIOS FOR CREATING COOPERATION IN THE CLASSROOM

Scenario: A student finishes an art project and leaves papers and markers on the desk and floor.

Parent Voice: *You're not leaving this room until that is all picked up!*

Child Voice: *Why can't you keep this room clean?*

1. Describe the Problem

Adult Voice: *I see a lot of papers and markers on the desk and floor.*

    Scenario: A student is standing on a chair.

    Parent Voice: *Get off the chair!*

    Child Voice: *These chairs are going to get ruined.*

2. Give Information

    Adult Voice: *Chairs are not for standing on.*

    Scenario: A student doesn't have a pencil.

    Parent Voice: *How many times do you need to be told to bring a pencil to class?*

    Child Voice: *I don't know what to do with you.*

3. Offer a Choice

    Adult Voice: *You can borrow a pencil from someone in the class or buy one from me.*

    Scenario: A student calls another student stupid.

    Parent Voice: *If you say that again, you're going to the office.*

    Child Voice: *Why do you have to call him names?*

4. Describe How You Feel

    Adult Voice: *I don't like hearing that word in this class.*

Avoiding power struggles with defiant students is the key to inviting cooperation. The more orders you give, the more resistant they will become. Precious instructional time can be wasted dealing with defiance and resistance. The goals of communicating cooperation are encouraging students to think about the problem and to behave more responsibly. When teachers invite cooperation, their students are more likely to change their behavior.

OFFERING CHOICES—WITHIN LIMITS

An assistant principal once told me what happened when he invited a defiant student to cooperate by acknowledging feelings and offering him a choice within limits.

> One of the aspects of my job that I don't like is being called upon to play "the heavy." Today one of the teachers called the office asking me to please come to the classroom and "do something" about Robert, who was refusing to leave the room. As I was walking to the classroom, I wondered what I would do if he refused to comply with my demand short of carrying him out of the room. When I entered the room, I saw Robert standing in the back of the classroom looking out the window with his teacher saying, "I told you I was going to call the office."
>
> I slowly walked up to Robert and quietly said, "Looks like there's a problem with you and the teacher. I'm surprised because you usually do well in this class." Robert said, "Not today. She told me to sit next to Frank who I can't stand." I said, "So it looks like you were just trying to stay out of more trouble. Let's talk about this outside. Should we leave out the back door or the front one?" Robert got his back pack and walked out the front door. I don't know who was more relieved—me or Robert.

We all understand that a vital goal of teaching is getting students to cooperate. As illustrated in the scenario above, teachers and administrators can get even defiant students to cooperate when they remember to provide choices throughout the day. My two-year-old daughter, Karta, was given a "tippy-top" glass of juice to prevent spills. She immediately began to cry because she didn't want the "tippy top." My response to her was, "Karta, you can have the cup with a top on it or I can put it in the refrigerator until you are ready. What do you want?" She stopped crying and in a quiet voice said, "With a top." The incident was over.

There are times when teachers think they are in control, but actually the student has regained control on their terms. For example, Ananda is talking outside the classroom when she should be in class. The teacher orders her to come in immediately. Ananda regains control by walking into the room as slowly as possible and, once she is in the classroom, begins talking to another student instead of sitting down and getting her assignment out. I think you can imagine where this can go from here. There is a basic rule in psychology that says, "I either give the other person control on my terms, or he will take it on his terms." This is true in the classroom with students as well as with our children at home. The power of giving choices within limits can be the difference between going home exhausted at the end of a work day or feeling uplifted by the ability to effect change in your students' behavior.

When does giving choices not work? It can be a problem when you are upset and cannot "think clearly." It is always best to give choices when you see a potential problem but the emotion and drama have not materialized. The general rule of giving choices is to do so when you are feeling good and everything is going smoothly. It's always more effective when we can be proactive versus reactive. Being proactive and not reactive puts you in control—insisting on and assisting in pro-moting appropriate behavior in a calm, profes-sional manner.

> You'd rather give students control on your terms than have students taking control on theirs.

If you find yourself reacting to a situation, analyze the situation, know what options you have, and execute them so that a minimum of disruption to learning time takes place. There are times when you, as the leader, need to make the choice for the student or class. These times include during an emergency, if someone may get hurt or time does not permit it. But your students will be much more agreeable when these times do arise if they sense that control is shared by the teacher. The fol-lowing guidelines when offering choices will also increase the important feeling of control-sharing in the classroom.

Guidelines for Providing Choices

- Whenever possible, provide choices you will be able to live with.
- Give choices only if you are willing and able to allow the student to experience the logical consequence of their choice.
- If a student cannot or will not make a choice within ten seconds, then you need to make the choice for that student.
- State choices in a neutral manner using words such as
  - Would you rather . . . or . . . ?
  - What would work for you, . . . or . . . ?
  - You're welcome to . . . or . . .

Examples of Offering Choices Within Limits

- "This project needs to be completed before the vacation. Would you rather make the deadline Thursday or Friday of next week?"
- "We can either walk to the bus together while walking in a straight line or I could dismiss you individually. It's up to you."

- "Would you rather follow the rules and participate or watch the others for a while? Let me know what you want to do."
- "Feel free to join us after you complete the assignment."
- "You're welcome to work cooperatively with this group or work by yourself. What would you prefer?"
- "What would work for you: finishing the project after school or doing it for homework?"
- "You can use crayons or magic markers."
- "You can either write an essay or a poem, it's your choice."

The proactive power of giving a student some of your control establishes an expectation of problem ownership. Teachers report that giving students full ownership of their problems through the use of choices within limits increases instructional time rather than wasting time enforcing rules. Consider what it would be like in your classroom if everyone exercised self-control. Offering a choice can establish an

Making a Choice?

overall feeling of satisfaction on the part of the student. Thinking through a situation brings a settling effect and a genuine interest in self-control.

I was observing a teacher conduct his lesson in a ninth-grade classroom when Laurie, who was talking, refused to sit at the front of the class when asked. I intervened to avoid a standoff between Laurie and the math teacher. I asked Laurie to step outside the classroom with me because I had an important question to ask her. She looked down at her books for a few moments and then decided to walk out into the hall.

Me: *What got you so upset?*

Student: *I don't like sitting in the front. I never sit in the front.*

Me: *Why did Mr. Rosever ask you to move to the front?*

Student: *I was talking.*

Me: *Well, what are your options?*

Student: *Go to Civility (in-house suspension room) for the day or move my seat.*

At that moment, Kevin McCaskill, the school principal, happened to be walking down the hall and I asked him to come over and join us.

Me: *Mr. McCaskill, Laurie has a choice to make. What do you think would be the wise decision?*

Principal: *Sounds like a no-brainer to me. Spend a day bored in Civility or stay in the classroom and get educated? I think you know what choice I'd make.*

Mr. McCaskill smiled and walked away, leaving the student's self-concept in place by giving her the time and space to make a choice. I told Laurie that I would watch to see what choice she made, and we walked into the classroom together. Laurie got her books and found a seat at the front of the classroom. I approached her after class and asked why she had decided to move. She said, "Civility is boring, and Mr. Rosever would probably make a big deal after class if I didn't."

I have found in most cases that, if we offer them a sufficient amount of time, students will come to the same conclusion an adult would. This student became less defiant and agitated because she was forced to think and own the consequence of her decision. Once thinking begins, rational behavior soon follows.

If Laurie had made the wrong choice by refusing to move, that would have been fine as well. We want our students to make mistakes and learn from the experience. If Laurie sat back down in her seat and refused to move, at the end of class the teacher would empathize, "I feel bad that you decided not to move because I know Civility is a boring place to spend a day. I'll look forward to having you back Thursday and sitting where I asked you to sit." This empathetic unstated message is one of belief that Laurie is wise enough to learn from the mistake she made. By not reacting, and therefore becoming emotionally involved with the student's wrong choice, the teacher would be allowing Laurie to experience the consequences of her actions. I once overheard a teacher tell her students, "Feel free to make mistakes, just make different ones." Students are most likely to make "different" mistakes when they are allowed to experience the logical consequences of their poor choices.

ACADEMIC CHOICE

Seventh-grade English teacher Ms. Contaste completed her lesson on autobiography with her mixed-ability special and general education students. Some of her students are reading at a lower grade level and others are gifted. Josh, George, and Rose resist writing and often refuse to participate. For this lesson, Ms. Contaste decided to use an instructional strategy called Academic Choice that she had learned in a workshop in *The Responsive Classroom* (Crawford & Wood, 1999). To stimulate thought about the topic being taught, and to promote active participation, she facilitated questions from all of her students. She then explained the assigned project and the means used to assess their performance during and after completing the project. One unique aspect of this strategy is the choice of work options. Students were offered a choice of a variety of approaches that would represent what they had learned (e.g., poetry, essay, photo album, video, drawing, song). They could work independently, with partners, or in cooperative groups. Ms. Contaste listed the materials to be used and set a deadline for the project. Understanding that interest increases focus on the activity, she integrated academic choice into her lessons. Ms. Contaste also challenged her students by saying, "This next project might be a little difficult—I hope you'll be able to complete it." Challenging some students makes them more interested in what is going on, and behavior problems may be reduced.

She kept students on task by observing, interacting, and asking questions to extend the quality of the project. After a few days, students presented either completed or work-in-progress projects while their peers and

Ms. Contaste provided constructive feedback. I observed learners who were engaged and therefore feeling in control and motivated to behave. Giving students a choice of how they could demonstrate their learning, and with whom they wanted to work, supported ownership of the learning process and provided many opportunities to explore their interests and strengths. Providing academic choice offered these students an opportunity to find their own special "voice." When students feel successful at their work, they are less inclined to misbehave.

AVOIDING POWER STRUGGLES

Thinking about the statement you make before making it can avoid unnecessary power struggles. Sometimes communicating choices can be more subtle in the message but can have the same power of change. Statements that are time consuming and usually unenforceable should be avoided. For example, I've heard a teacher make the statement "We will all sit here until everyone is quiet" a few minutes before the last bell rang. I watched as some of the students who were in a teacher-student power struggle tested the teacher's resolve. The class was eventually dismissed so students could get on the bus. The statement was time consuming and unenforceable. A subtle choice which gives you control as to when it will be enforced is always preferable—for example, "I'll be asking you to line up as soon as it's quiet." Table 3.2 presents some examples of subtle choice statements which avoid power struggles while enabling students to cooperate and feel in control.

SETTING LIMITS THROUGH THINKING WORDS

How do we promote quality thinking in the classroom? Change will only happen through quality questions. For example, teachers who utilize Bloom's Taxonomy of the Cognitive Domain (Bloom, 1976) are committed to giving their students practice with extended thinking skills. When a student is engaged in higher level thinking, they feel better about who they are as a learner.

> Teachers can inspire different results from students with a single change in the habitual questions they ask.

Anthony Robbins (1994) points out that quality questions create a quality life. He believes that the questions you ask consistently create either indignation or inspiration. I have found that using "thinking" rather than "shrinking" words will inspire students to be responsible rather than reactionary.

Table 3.2   Statements for Avoiding Power Struggles and Enabling Students

Possible Power Struggle	Enforceable
"No, you can't sharpen your pencil."	"Pencils can be sharpened when I'm not giving directions."
"Stop bothering Jessie!"	"You're welcome to sit next to Jessie as long as you can keep your hands to yourself."
"Take out your books now and open them to page 78."	"We'll be starting on page 78 in the blue book."
"Don't expect a good grade if you hand the assignment in late."	"I always give full credit for assignments that are handed in on time."
"I don't lend out pencils. You should bring in your own."	"Feel free to ask a classmate for a pencil."
"Stop shouting out answers!"	"I'm glad to see that you're excited about answering my questions, but I call on students who raise their hands."
"Go to time out."	"You're welcome to work quietly with us or you can sit in the time-out area until you're ready to cooperate."

Thinking Words Versus Shrinking Words

Setting limits through thinking words may take time and practice. Remember, sometimes we have old communication habits that need to be broken as well. We understand that limits are important because they determine the boundaries in which a safe and secure environment can exist. But we often confuse limit setting with ordering or giving commands. Laying down emotional ultimatums only shrinks a student's self-concept, causing them to make angry decisions. Our ongoing challenge is setting limits without waging wars. Words that create wars and deflate self-concept tell students what the teacher will do to make them comply. Thinking words establish the same limit, but tell students how the teacher will act. It is important to differentiate between these two statements.

Setting a limit is inherent in the statements you make, as well as the questions you ask a student. It means asking students to make a choice on your terms rather than taking control on theirs. Making statements that use thinking words will facilitate the thinking versus reacting process. The examples of thinking words versus shrinking words in Table 3.3 exemplify the choices you can offer in the classroom.

Table 3.3   Shrinking and Thinking Words

Shrinking Words	Thinking Words
"You'll be getting an 'F' in my class."	"You can pass this class if you begin handing in some completed work for me to grade. Does this sound reasonable to you?"
"No wonder you don't have any friends. You're always making fun of other kids."	"You might be the first student at Kennedy that can make friends by calling them names, but I've never seen someone make friends that way."
"You're not coming to the assembly with that type of behavior."	"Feel free to join us for this afternoon's assembly as long as you can follow the classroom respect rules."

THE CRITICISM TRAP

With good intentions, teachers often ask students questions that either put them on the defensive or diminish their self-esteem. For example, have you noticed that, after a student misbehaves and is asked the question, "Why did you do that?" the answer is usually, "I don't know." Students unconsciously attempt to distance themselves from the question and therefore the incident, avoiding responsibility. Asking "why" is usually ineffective. At one time, asking "why" was a form of genuine inquiry, but now this question is interpreted as "why in the world are you so stupid?" Asking "why" questions only creates resentment and confusion inside the student. Teachers will fall into a cycle of criticism by asking poor quality questions that begin with a critical comment such as, "What trouble did you get into today" or "What have you done now?" Questions like these create feelings of inadequacy and avoidance of responsibility. It is true that children learn what they live. A student who learns to be kind to others has been treated with kindness and compassion. If students who are having problems with behaving in class live with criticism, they do not learn responsibility but instead begin to feel bad about themselves and to find fault with others. When a parent criticizes their child for misbehaving, it is just a matter of time until that child finds fault with another person in the family or at school. As I

> Our questions could either improve our students' future or block their future improvement.

illustrated in Chapter 2, these negative cycles gain power and perpetuate their own false reality. The cycles of reinforcing attitudes and behaviors will continue if an adult doesn't intervene.

Lesson Box 3.1   Detention With Dignity

Many high school teachers become frustrated with using the consequence of a detention for reasons that include students not showing up because they forget, thinking that nothing will happen if they do not show up, or believing they are being treated unfairly. Any discipline intervention that doesn't preserve a student's dignity and self-esteem will not educate the student. I worked with a new and very talented first-year high school English teacher, Sarah Akhtar, on an adapted detention procedure that would meet the requirements I believe are necessary for teaching discipline. This is an example of a teacher who takes her responsibility of managing a classroom seriously. The following is her description of the problem and the solution that was implemented.

The Problem

Students were not showing up for detentions. Often, the problem was not being followed up by administration, so the teacher had no reinforcement or negative consequences.

I Tried . . .

Making lists of names on a board of students who had detention. However, students were still not showing up.

SiriNam Khalsa pointed out to me that the students might feel embarrassed or upset by having their name on the "detention list" for all to see, and therefore not come. Another approach was needed.

The Solution

I made little notices that I now hand out to students as soon as a detention is assigned. For example:

You, _____ , have detention with Ms. Akhtar at 2:05 p.m. You have been assigned detention for the following reason(s):

a. Excessive tardiness

b. Classroom misconduct

c. Failure to do assignments

d. Other: _____

If you do not come to your detention, you will receive office detention, then three days of in-house suspension. The choice is yours. If you cannot make the above date, I need a note **signed by a parent** explaining why not, with a phone number I can call to schedule a better time for you.

Thank you,

Ms. Akhtar

The note is given discreetly so that the student does not "lose face" in front of his or her peers. If the detention is scheduled for the following week, I give a small reminder notice (a quarter-page):

This is a reminder that you, _____, have a detention on _____. Please show up promptly at 2:05 p.m. and bring a writing implement. Thank you.

Outcome

Suddenly, five or six students were showing up for detention right at 2:05 p.m.!

Next Goal

Not needing to assign so many detentions!

We want students to trust their own judgment, and to develop the ability to trust the intentions of others. I can usually pick distrustful students out in a classroom. They have a persona that reflects an expectation of impending doom. To break this cycle of criticism and distrust, ask a question in such a way that a student focuses on the question rather then the emotional content or baggage. We want to encourage thinking, and therefore students who engage in the process of problem solving. Table 3.4 presents some examples illustrating how asking a student a quality question can change a negative cycle.

Table 3.4   Negative Verses Positive Cycle Questions

Instead of . . .	Ask . . .
"What did you do this time?"	"What could you learn from what happened?"
"Why are you always the last one in line?"	"How can you get in line a little sooner?"
"Do you think I'm going to believe that?"	"Is there anything else you might need to tell me?"
"Why can't you just do what I ask?"	"What do you think it would be like if you followed my directions?"
"Don't tell me, you didn't do your homework again?"	"What needs to happen for you to get homework in on time?"

Quality questions empower the student to problem solve and improve their situation. We want to help students to change their old negative cycles of reinforcing attitudes and behaviors by asking questions that do not highlight their disabilities but rather tap into their abilities. We are constantly asking students questions, but remember: it isn't only the questions you ask them, but the questions you don't ask them, that shape their future.

Strategies Impacting Positive Discipline and Self-Respect

TIME OUT

Placing a student into an area that can be used for "time out"—sometimes referred to as "thinking time"—can be a good strategy to use in the classroom if it is handled properly. Unfortunately, however, I have witnessed the abuse of time out in too many classrooms. To begin with, the term "time out" seems to have taken on a negative connotation because of the possible abuses of this intervention. I've used and heard other teachers substitute alternative terms such as "thinking time," the "thinking chair," or the "critical thinking area." One science teacher even had a large photo of the moon on the partition that separated the time-out corner from the room. The students in her classroom named their time-out area "the Moon," and when they needed time away from the class, they were asked to go to "the Moon." I refer to this strategy as "thinking time" because it should be emphasized that it is a think-it-over place away from other students.

One way in which thinking time has been abused by teachers is its use in escalating a power struggle. Teachers can do this by saying, "Go to time out until I tell you to come back." Or, "You stay in time out until your work is finished." It usually takes just a few minutes for most students to get themselves together. When put in time out for half an hour or longer, a student has plenty of time to plan how to get revenge—and so the power struggle begins.

The Forgotten Child

When I began teaching and did not understand the appropriate use of time out, I learned a big lesson from a relatively small mistake. I had sent a boy to time out with the instruction to stay there until I thought he was ready to return to class. An hour later, I realized I had forgotten that he was still in time out, so I went back for him. I found him writing with pen every curse word imaginable on the door, desk, walls, and chair. He was quietly using his time not to think over why he was there, but how to get

The Forgotten Child

back at me for banishing him from class. The damage was done and it created a whole new problem that had to be dealt with.

Looking back on the situation, I realize that this boy probably would have been ready to return to class in five minutes, so he had fifty-five minutes left to become more negative. Thinking time is not a punishment and should not be confused with anything similar that is used as a negative reinforcer. If a young elementary-aged child is pushing a peer, the teacher needs to say, "Joshua, I cannot have you pushing Alex, so I think you need some thinking time. Please sit in the thinking chair for five minutes. I will let you know when the five minutes are up." (Some teachers prefer to let the student decide when they are ready to return to the group.)

Thinking time is a versatile discipline technique that needs to be administered in as calm, collected, and prompt a manner as possible. It can be used with two students, by putting each in a separate corner or different room. I've even seen teachers use thinking time with three and four students at once. It is especially helpful for bickering and teasing among peers, who will quickly escalate the behavior without early intervention.

Guidelines for the Thinking Time

1. Make a place within the classroom for thinking time. Creative use of partitions, desks, or other furniture can often create the necessary visual barrier away from peers.

2. Let the student be in charge (within reason) of when to come back to class unless a thinking time planning form needs to be filled out.

3. Do not send class work to thinking time with the student. A self-reflection questionnaire can be effective in helping students to understand the cycle they need to change.

4. For most students, counseling is not necessary after returning from thinking time.

5. If a student prefers to sit alone in thinking time for large amounts of time, that student may need professional counseling. Some problems cannot effectively be dealt with in the classroom setting.

Buddy Room

When thinking time does not help the student change the behavior that initially created the problem, an alternative action is needed. Standing in the hall outside the classroom is not advisable because the student is not being supervised. In one middle school, a procedure which often has positive results involves the use of a "buddy room." If a student who is repeatedly sent to thinking time comes back and starts acting up again, then that student is escorted to another teacher's classroom for the remainder of the period. Before this occurs, you can say, "You're in a quiet, thinking-it-over place, and we do have the buddy room to go to if that's necessary." Teachers make an agreement to use each other's rooms for the extended thinking time area. This more intense level of thinking time away from their peers and teacher can be effective when the student understands that they are welcome to return to class if they are really ready to change their behavior.

If acting out continues in the "buddy room," then an administrator is called to escort the student to the office for a more severe consequence— which may include a call home to a parent or an in-school suspension. If a parent is called, the teacher who placed the student in the "buddy room" should be involved in problem solving with the student and parent(s).

Middle and High School Thinking Time

After many years as a middle school teacher, working at the high school level has given me new insights on how high school–aged students think and feel. Thinking time at the high school level takes a very different form. Because of the natural stage of development in adolescence, high school students do not want to feel forced to do anything or they rebel and may become more defiant. Respectful dialogue is the key to working out thinking time issues.

Teacher: *Sandra, I must admit your constant talking is getting to me. Please feel free to be somewhere else if you cannot control your need to talk when we're working.*

Sandra: *Okay, I need to be somewhere else. I might be back.*

For this dialogue to be able to take place, high school teachers and administrators need to create an acceptable place for students to be when they are not in the classroom. Often the only alternative is standing in the hallway or being sent to the office.

High school–aged students are similar to middle school students in that they like teachers who try to understand them and offer help when they ask for it. They want teachers who respond to them as people, and demonstrate a genuine caring attitude by treating them with respect regardless of their behavior.

The teachers who bark out military-style orders to "Sit down," "Be quiet," or "Get out and go to the office," are usually most disliked. High school–aged students definitely don't like people whose sole purpose seems to be to force them to act in a certain way. This poses a unique challenge when teaching in a high school. Students who are repeatedly disruptive already think school is not for them. It is therefore essential to be aware of the repeating negative cycles they have created. Students often look for the negative comment which keeps this cycle going. Their self-image is damaged, and they have a tendency to listen for comments teachers make that confirm

> The bottom line for all students is that they don't care how much you know until they know how much you care.

their view of themselves. We know that the teacher is the key to changing these negative behavior and attitude cycles. When we are able to have alternative arrangements for thinking time as well as respectful dialogue with all our students, thinking time can become a strategy for reducing the negative feelings they have toward school and teachers.

Enhancing the effectiveness of thinking time, especially with certain students at the elementary and middle school levels, can require students to own their problem and solution by writing down answers to the following four questions:

1. What did I do?

2. Did I break a rule?

3. What will I do next time?

4. What is a fair consequence if this happens again?

Explain to your students that the thinking time area is used for "thinking of a better way to control their behavior." The thinking time planning form (see Activity Sheet 4.1) is a way to help students reflect on the behavior that got them there through specific questions that need to be answered. Some teachers use this form as a means of demonstrating the student's readiness to rejoin the class. For others it is a means of collecting information that can be discussed at a later time. I have found this form useful for my record keeping. When a student is continually being sent to thinking time, this form can be used to review with the student. If we want children to assume responsibility for their actions and to perceive a rule as being fair, they must reflect on the above questions.

Gerald was asked to sit in thinking time during his math class. His teacher asked whether I could talk to Gerald about his negative behavior cycle. When I read the thinking time planning form he had filled out, I was intrigued by his response. He said the reason he sits in thinking time is because he is protesting the rules that the teacher

Activity Sheet 4.1   The Thinking Time Planning Form

Name _____

Date _____

The rules for this thinking time area are very important and must be followed. Remember that your teacher cares about you, but right now he or she must pay attention to other students.

1.   Stay seated quietly while in the thinking time area. Raise your hand if you have an emergency and wait to be recognized.

2.   Answer the following questions. It is important that you give thoughtful answers.

My Plan

1.   What did I do?

_____
_____
_____
_____

2.   Did I break a rule? If so, what rule?

_____
_____
_____
_____

3.   What will I do next time?

_____
_____
_____
_____

4.   What is a fair consequence if this happens again?

_____
_____
_____
_____

has created. I asked him if he would make different class rules if he could. Gerald thought for a moment and said, "Maybe. But I don't like always being told what to do." I probably would have not received this information if it were not for the planning form.

During the "orientation" period I suggest is used for the first week of school, it is important to ask students what rules they think are necessary and what would be the best ways to remember these rules so that the teacher doesn't have to remind them. I also encourage teachers to ask students about the most effective consequences should the rules be broken. This conversation can act as a catalyst for ownership and group responsibility. As in Gerald's case, I find that many students are more likely to remember and follow rules that they have helped to create, since they feel a greater sense of ownership for these rules.

REPEATING

This strategy is also referred to by Canter and Canter (1976) as the "broken-record technique." Repeating is used when a student is not acknowledging your statement. Teachers have the right to expect their students to listen to them. Some students who have emotional or learning disabilities are unaware that they are not "hearing" what the teacher is saying. Repeating acknowledges this situation and offers a simple way to send the message, "I understand but listen to what I'm saying." This is done by repeating a statement to which a student seems not to be responding.

When using the repeating strategy, it is especially helpful to interject a dose of empathy. Empathy with repeating drives home the message that the teacher cares for the student, but the student needs to learn how to listen the first time something is stated. This can be accomplished by following these guidelines:

- Before repeating the statement, preface it with a statement that communicates your understanding of what the student is saying.
- Establish eye contact with the student before repeating the statement while using a respectful but firm tone of voice.
- To avoid a power struggle, do not repeat your statement more than three times.
- When the student complies, thank them for listening and then quickly move on.

I observed a skillful sixth-grade teacher using the repeating strategy in the school gym while students were supposed to be lining up to go to lunch.

Teacher:	*Joseph, when it's time to line up, give me the ball and line up.*
Joseph:	*I was supposed to shoot the ball next and Peter took the ball away from me so I grabbed it and tried to shoot.*
Teacher:	*Peter took the ball out of your hands. I understand that but when it's time to line up, hand the ball to me.*
Joseph:	*I didn't get my turn. He grabbed the ball from me.*
Teacher:	*I'll talk to Peter about that later. But remember when it's time to line up, give me the ball and get into line. Thanks for listening. Now let's get in line.*

REDIRECTING

I always understood that redirecting a young child's energy was effective, but how effective was it for older children and adolescents? There are certain students who have developed a negative outlook toward learning and consequently will avoid any direct involvement in a lesson. They seem to take up space in the classroom when they are there and are usually labeled troublemakers. Using direct confrontation is ineffective or imprudent with such a student. Redirecting can be very effective with certain students, especially those who need encouragement to engage in the learning process but tend to pull the teacher into "criticism traps." This strategy helps the student to turn their attention to something productive and instructive. The following lesson illustrates my point.

> José is a big boy who was retained in ninth grade. He's usually in trouble, rarely in class, and in private teachers call him "lazy José." He seems to have no roots, home or school. His internal guidance is unstable, with no goal of graduating. Beneath the uncaring rebel seems to lie a confused teenager who wants to obtain the competencies taught in class and to feel part of the school community.
>
> I was coteaching a lesson and facilitating cooperative learning groups with a ninth-grade math teacher. When the math teacher put a warm-up problem on the board, all the students began working except for José. Instead he began looking around the room for someone to bother or with whom to engage in a conversation. A simple authority move might call for the math teacher to tell José to "take your pencil out and get to work." I did not know José but knew other students with similar behavior cycles. I used a redirecting strategy by walking up to José and asking him whether he understood the assignment. He looked up at me and

said, "Yeah. But I don't have anything to write with." I took out a pen from my jacket pocket and said, "This is my favorite pen and I don't lend it out. Will you remember to return it?" José responded, "Sure I will" and began writing down the problem.

José stopped working after he wrote down the problem. I noticed him looking over another student's shoulder. I walked up to him again and asked if he needed help. He said he was lost. I then asked the student whose shoulder he was looking over if he understood how to solve the problem and asked if he would help José, which he did. After a few minutes, I approached José and asked whether he now understood the problem. He explained to me how he got his answer.

As the students completed the warm-up exercise, I noticed José beginning to get off task again by talking to someone across the room. I quickly decided the next redirecting strategy called for me to get José more involved in the lesson by asking him to come up to the board and solve the problem for the class. He was visibly surprised (as were the other students and teacher) and responded with, "I'm too fat and lazy to come to the board." Without losing a beat I said, "You might think you're too fat and lazy, but I still want you to write your answer on the board." He, as well as some other students, laughed at my response. José also knew I wasn't backing down so he slowly got out of his seat, brushed himself off, and came to the board. I gave him a piece of chalk and directed him to the section of the chalkboard he could write on. I then asked two other students to come to the board as well. This took the attention off José.

After this activity, the math teacher divided the students into groups of four. They were given assignments and a time limit in which the answers needed to be completed. I asked José to be the "product manager" of his group. He accepted and they began to work. The math teacher and I both circulated among the groups for the remainder of the class. José needed occasional prompting to stay on task during the lesson, but in general he was engaged and cooperating with his peers. At the end of class I thanked him for his participation as he thanked me for lending him my pen.

José's engagement in the lesson became the goal of using this strategy. Redirecting his energy toward productive purposes called attention to what he was doing correctly while his misbehavior became smaller and more manageable. A positive behavior cycle was created; however, for José to see himself as a competent student who can behave and learn with his peers, this positive cycle would need to be reinforced every day in math class. Giving feedback such as "Thanks for participating" also acted as a catalyst for changing unproductive behavior. For the effects of this positive experience to take hold, José would need to attend class regularly and have more successful learning experiences. At that point, a new attitude and behavior cycle can replace the old one.

MOMENTUM

The effective teacher is conscious of the many pitfalls that can disrupt the smooth, consistent flow or momentum of events in the classroom. When the inevitable distractions occur, the effective teacher will try to ignore them by staying on target, completing the task at hand, and "protecting" the working environments of students who are actively engaged. Saphier and Gower (1990) point out that "when momentum is not maintained, students get bored or look for things to do, potentially filling their time by daydreaming or engaging in disruptive behavior" (p. 31). Conversely, when the teacher maintains the momentum of a lesson, students are involved in a smooth transition from one event to another. Anticipating incidents that may break the momentum and making decisions that will avoid interruptions are integral to keeping the class moving along. The following two scenarios illustrate the power of losing and maintaining the momentum of a lesson.

Lost Momentum

In a high school English class I observed, the teacher was first interrupted by two students coming to the door selling roses for a fundraiser. It took several minutes for the teacher to realize no one was going to buy a rose and that he was losing the class. After spending more time getting everyone refocused, he noticed someone in the back of the classroom writing in a textbook. He stopped the lesson, walked to the back of the classroom and delivered a three-minute lecture on the importance of respecting school property. While this was going on, the rest of the students became restless. Some of the students closed their texts while others began talking and laughing. A few students decided to drop out by putting their heads down.

I'm not suggesting that the inappropriate behavior shouldn't have been dealt with, but it was obvious that the flow of the lesson was lost and the classroom management eventually fell apart. If the teacher walked to the back of the classroom while continuing the lesson and made a gesture to the student signaling his awareness of the offense, most likely the student would have stopped writing in the book while the momentum of the lesson continued. The behavior and its consequence could have been postponed until the end of class, and the students who came to the door could have been quickly and politely asked to return at the end of class as well.

Maintaining Momentum

I encourage teachers to have students work in cooperative groups as much as possible. However, there are a variety of momentum stoppers that can occur when groups are formed and students are actively interacting with each other. We divided a ninth-grade algebra class into five learning groups. The math teacher was working with one group and noticed that a couple of students in another group at the other end of the room were not working. Instead, they were laughing and discussing sports. The math teacher made sure the group he was working with was on track and told them he would check their answers in a few minutes. He then quickly and quietly walked across the room to the other group with the students who were joking around and delivered a soft reprimand: "Both of you need to stop talking about sports and either help your team solve the problem or work individually. I'll be back in a few minutes to see how you've contributed to this group's work."

Teachers who maintain momentum are able to work with individual students or small groups and keep the class focused on the task while at the same time dealing with inappropriate behavior. Being able to "multitask," or handle more than one thing at a time by giving attention to each event, is an essential component of maintaining momentum in today's differentiated classrooms. I once explained this reality to a group of teachers and one person said, "But what if we were never taught how to multitask?" I explained that some aspects of becoming an effective teacher take time, but with focused awareness and experimentation, positive changes can occur. The same teacher responded, "What if we've been teaching in a certain way and do not want to change but expect the students to change?" At that point my response was short and to the point: "I can only say what I have found to work in today's classrooms. Teaching in a mixed-ability classroom is for anyone but not for everyone."

Unfortunately, some teachers view their profession as a "job" and are preoccupied with work hours and vacation time. A professional teacher is willing to put in the necessary time and effort to improve themselves, their coworkers and their students. To become an effective teacher of discipline, one must become a risk taker, a problem solver, and a decision maker. Becoming proficient in a strategy such as multitasking will take effort and a certain amount of risk taking.

Multitasking is also referred to as overlapping (Kounin, 1970). It involves expanding your attention while keeping the focus on the lesson's objective. Circulating among your students while watching what is occurring in all corners of the room will keep students on task and disruptions to a minimum because you will be able to notice and respond to misbehavior in its early stages.

The following is an example of a middle school art teacher multitasking to maintain class momentum.

> Across the room, a student appears frustrated with a pencil sharpener. While helping one student with the assignment, the teacher says, "Susan, ask Karen if you need some help sharpening the pencil." The teacher notices another student completing his project and says, "Alex, did you design a border for the drawing?" Alex replies, "Yes. It's on the back shelf." The teacher responds, "Great. After you complete the project you can read the book you brought to class." The teacher had anticipated a need for a filler activity to keep the student on task for the remainder of the class. Another student is seen finishing her project and the jar of paint she is using. The teacher reminds her to refill the paint jar when she's finished and asks her to refill the other jars if there is time before the end of class.

The decisions this art teacher made kept potential disruptions to the lesson's momentum to a minimum. While working with individual students and small groups, and having an active role in the teaching of the large group, the teacher kept the flow of the lesson going. Decisions were made without interrupting or moving attention from the primary learning objective. This is an example of masterful teaching which often looks easy but it isn't. I use the analogy of watching an accomplished dancer moving gracefully around the stage with no visible tension. Probably most important, this teacher is the kind of person who is willing to try new strategies and make the personal commitment to become involved as a change agent for the students.

SELF-MONITORING CHECKLIST

The self-monitoring checklist (see Activity Sheet 4.2) is based on the premise that students need to feel a certain amount of control in their daily lives. Many of the symptoms that get labeled as misbehavior in the classroom are actually students looking for some degree of control over others due to a lack of self-control. This phenomenon is often evident in interactions between students and their teachers and parents or guardians. When these control issues escalate into power struggles, they become draining to all of us who are involved.

The self-monitoring checklist is just one more tool that may be helpful in your overall plan for teaching discipline. I have seen immediate change in behavior after implementing this strategy, especially with students who are emotionally needy and demonstrative in their lack of control. This strategy shares control and gives the student the responsibility for demonstrating their own progress.

I suggest trying this intervention with a few students who express the desire to take on the responsibility of filling out the form. Self-monitoring can be used every day for a few weeks and then intermittently given to the student as needed. It is not unusual for a student to show immediate progress for a few days, regress into old behaviors for a day or two, and then return to the improved behavior.

How to Use Self-Monitoring

The steps involved when implementing this strategy are as follows.

1. Explain to the student that he or she will be responsible for filling out the form at the end of each class, period, or day. Some teachers use this at the end of classes that are most problematic (e.g., physical education and recess, or Spanish and math).

2. Give the student full responsibility for asking the teacher to sign the form at the end of the class or day. If the teacher disagrees with the student's self-evaluation, they can discuss the issue at that time and come to a mutual agreement.

3. Collect the forms. At the end of the week, they can be sent home to a parent and new expectations can be set for the following week. Some teachers attach reinforcers (e.g., privileges or awards) when progress is demonstrated.

Activity Sheet 4.2   Self-Monitoring Checklist

Self-Monitoring Checklist

Name _____

Date _____ Subject _____

Check "Yes" or "No" at the end of class.

Today I . . .	Yes	No
Quietly walked into the classroom.		
Stayed in my seat.		
Did my class work.		
Didn't distract anyone else.		
Listened to the teacher.		

How many times did you check "Yes"? _____

How many times did you check "No"? _____

_____

Teacher's Signature _____

SOURCE: Adapted with permission from S. Khalsa (2005). *The Inclusive Classroom.* Tucson, AZ: Good Year Books.

SELF-CONTROL CARDS

This strategy was first shared with me by a high school English teacher, Sarah Akhtar. We both benefit from finding the time to sit together and share the challenges and successes we are experiencing in the classroom. I believe teachers should seek out other teachers who have complementary teaching styles and temperaments. Taking the opportunity to share experiences with your colleagues can inspire you to stay abreast of current ideas in your field, open new doors to old problems, and bring forth a renewed sense of enthusiasm.

This intervention can be extremely effective and takes little effort and time on the teachers' part. Its effectiveness is based on the understanding that all students want some degree of control, and, as I mentioned earlier, you'd rather give students control on your terms then students taking control on theirs. This intervention also catches the student being good, which research clearly indicates is the most effective way of changing behavior.

Self-control cards (see Figure 4.1) have three colors: red, green, and white. If you laminate them, they will last for a long time. The red cards (stop) provide a way to intervene when minor or chronic behavior problems occur. For example, when a student taps his or her pencil one too

---

Privilege Card

Use this card for an extra privilege today.

Phone Call Home

If you change your behavior, I will take this card back.
If not, you will get a phone call home tonight.

Figure 4.1   Self-Control Cards

many times, or insists on talking instead of working, he or she is quietly given a card to read. The red card states, "Phone Call Home: If you change your behavior, I will take this card back. If not, you will get a phone call home tonight." The green cards provide a way to keep students on task and repeat the desired behavior. Green cards state, "5 Bonus Points! This card will add 5 bonus points on your next test or quiz." The white cards also provide a powerful incentive to change behaviors and maintain self-control. White cards state, "Got Ya! You've been caught being responsible. I will call home to give your parents the good news." This card is especially effective in helping students to change a chronic negative behavior cycle. Parents of these students are accustomed to receiving the "bad news" phone calls. I want to help these parents feel good about their children, and have opportunities to give these students praise and encouragement whenever possible. The impact is always more effective than continuous reprimanding for negative behavior.

A modified version of self-control cards is keeping a stack of cards with consequences written on them. When a student is continually not following a behavioral expectation, ask them to "pick a card . . . any card" and deliver the consequence. Possible consequences can include note home, lunch detention, clean desks, thinking time, loss of a privilege, and so on. Students who have a history of being defiant or hostile may be permitted to remove the card they consider most undesirable.

STAYING IN THE PRESENT

Being capable is more than academic achievement and success. Students also gain a sense of how capable they are by being in charge of their emotional lives—specifically, being able to control or change their thought processes by reframing them in a positive way. This process is not easy for many students, so they need adult support to help them see it is not so much the event that determines their behavior as how they think about it. Every feeling is preceded by a thought. For example, I noticed a student breaking his pencil in half while sitting in math class. When I asked him why he did this, he looked at me with an angry face and said, "Last night my little brother took my CDs and threw them in the toilet!" Recalling the incident produced the same emotions as if it had just happened in math class. We later had a discussion about the connection between thinking and behavior. I recommended visualizing a "stop sign" when he began thinking angry thoughts. The goal was to keep his thoughts, and consequently his behavior, in the present—not the past or the future. This mental stop sign is a signal to stop dysfunctional or unwanted thoughts.

Show and Don't Tell

Randy is a shy, introverted fourteen-year-old high school student who exhibits some repetitive autistic-type behaviors. His English teacher, Ms. Allowe, has difficulty getting any work out of him. Here is the first conversation she had with him:

Teacher: *Randy, I see you haven't done any work so far. Is there something you don't understand?*

Randy: *Nah. I understand. But I just . . . I'm finished.*

Teacher: *What do you mean you're finished? Don't you care about your work?*

Randy: *Why should I care? No one cares about me.*

Teacher: *I care about you, Randy. I care about you passing this year.*

Randy remains silent and continues to sulk. The teacher, with good intentions, tries to convince Randy that she cares but receives no response. Randy continues to do little or no work. Ms. Allowe is dealing with a student who has a poor self-image and low self-esteem. Trying to convince him that he is worthy of caring will not make an impact because he is not ready to see things differently. It is often more effective to show a student what you think rather than just telling them. Active listening, or reflecting Randy's statement that "no one cares" and then saying "that must feel really bad," would have helped Randy to feel understood. Ms. Allowe might next say, "I've felt that way before and it is a bad feeling. Now, how can I help you to get some work done?" Her caring behavior would be more believable than her words.

Lessons Needed to Be Learned

I began my career as an art teacher in a large suburban middle school in upstate New York. After getting my certification, I found myself interested in working with students who were on the periphery of the school community so I gravitated toward special education. My first teaching position as a special educator was in a residential school for adolescent boys who had severe emotional disabilities. My discipline strategies were based on overpowering the students. Being a new teacher, I mirrored those around me and these strategies seemed to work reasonably well.

In spite of my heavy-handed use of discipline, students liked me and I enjoyed teaching them. Then I got my first "hard-core" student—Ronnie.

Ronnie was different. He was quite unpredictable. Sometimes he would do what he was asked, and other times became so disruptive that he would need to be physically removed from the classroom. Ronnie seemed to act with no internal guidance system, grabbing things from other students, pushing and shoving, yelling and being combative. He was a student I found very difficult to like. My overpowering techniques didn't make the slightest difference to his behavior.

One day, Ronnie stuck a pencil in another student's arm. While lecturing him in the hallway with the school disciplinarian at my side, without warning Ronnie put his head down and punched me in the chest. As an unconscious reaction, I forcefully pushed him back, knocking him to the floor. I found myself holding my hand, which was in excruciating pain, while Ronnie got up, looked up at me, and said, "You can't hurt me. My father could never hurt me either." I'm certainly not proud of this. I had a few days to think about this incident while getting a hand cast for a broken bone in my thumb. This was a demoralizing experience for me, but it ultimately became a defining point in my teaching career. The school principal was very understanding and said he probably would have reacted in the same way. Despite this, I realized I needed to find a different school to work in if I was going to stay in this profession. This incident occurred about the same time that my family had decided to move to Massachusetts. I got a special education teaching position in a collaborative school. My quest for ways to control students continued.

I was hired as the head teacher in a class of students with a variety of emotional and learning disabilities. I approached my new challenge with renewed enthusiasm but was having difficulty with a student who had similar characteristics to Ronnie. Jason would also provoke other students to act out and then avoid any responsibility for his involvement. One day, with help from an assistant teacher, I needed to physically restrain Jason from hurting another student. After we let him go, Jason told me he was going to get his "friend" after me and ran out of the school building.

The next day during class, one of my students pointed to the door. Peering through the window was an angry young man's serious face. I asked my assistant to take over while I stepped outside the room to be greeted by a very large, angry young man wearing a camouflage outfit. He asked if I was the teacher who had grabbed his buddy Jason. I found myself at another defining point in my teaching career. At this point you might be asking yourself, "What would I have done in this situation?" Without thinking, I went into professional mode and said, "I'm very happy that you came in today. But in the future, please call the school to make an appointment. Since you are here, why don't we go to the office and meet." He nodded his head and followed me to the office. I asked him to please take a seat while I got an administrator. I immediately went into the principal's office and explained the situation. She told me I had done the correct thing by not trying to deal with situation alone. The principal called the police and the incident was resolved. It turned out that Jason's buddy was a twenty-year-old man from his neighborhood who had been involved with the court system for aggressive behavior.

Fortunately, I was young and in good physical shape, but the stress was taking a toll on my emotional body. Later during that year, the consulting school psychologist who occasionally visited my classroom offered me a book to read entitled *Between Teacher and Child* by Dr. Haim G. Ginott (1970). I was still teaching using the paradigm of controlling students. The reference to "communicating effectively by getting through to your student" attracted me since I was looking for a hands-off approach toward helping my students to comply with my wishes and be responsible for their own behavior.

I decided to become a student of Haim Ginott. For the rest of that year, I read nothing but his books, learning his approaches toward dealing with the whole student. I also used his effective communication strategies with the different ages and populations of students I eventually taught. Ginott's emphasis on the power of words sparked a deeper interest in me which was a catalyst for reaching and teaching all special and regular education students. I came to realize that teaching discipline was a complicated kindness—a science that needed to be practiced artfully.

At some point in my "mentorship" with Dr. Ginott, I realized I had never asked myself a fundamental question: Did I want to control my students or did I want to help them control themselves? The answer became very clear. I discovered that getting cooperation was not only more enjoyable, but was less stressful for both me and my students.

COLLABORATIVE TEAMING: MANY HEADS ARE BETTER THAN ONE

When I reflected on writing this book, one of the key ingredients I felt was necessary for teaching discipline was connecting through teamwork and collaboration among staff, parents, and community. In the teaching profession, the idea of working in teams in the same school or as partners in the same classroom makes good sense. It can provide a healthier, more balanced environment for everyone involved. Teaming gives educators an opportunity to extend their interpersonal skills. With more and more children who have significant behavioral and learning needs placed in the general education classroom, it is essential that teachers network with

Cooperating With Students

others who can help provide the necessary supports that allow students to succeed. Teaching discipline should not be a singular effort by one teacher. In fact, for success to prevail, classroom teachers need help and support to succeed—they cannot and should not be expected to do it alone.

Service Teams

There are countless collaborative models that are being experimented with in schools everywhere. In my school district, we implemented a "service team" model (COMPASS Consulting, 2005) which incorporates a great deal of collaboration among teachers, specialists, community members, and parents. The work of the service team focuses on solving problems that get in the way of academic achievement and social-emotional-behavioral development. The problem solving becomes a regular and integral part of the work of members on the teams. The service team develops and implements action plans which include clear objectives and time lines indicating when the objectives will be met. After communicating the action plan with others who work with the student, weekly evaluation of the objectives' progress is an integral aspect of this team model. Records of problem solving describe the work done by the teams in putting together action plans. At the end of the school year, or when a student leaves the school, records of problem solving are stored and available to staff and teams working with the student in the future. This assures continuity and support for building on what has been effective in the past. The outcome has been positive. In the last three years, hundreds of teachers have met in teams to develop action plans for thousands of students in elementary, middle, and, most recently, high schools.

A major challenge of service teams is keeping a focus on preventive interventions and conscious planning by a team of concerned people. A tendency for teachers who are feeling frustrated with difficult students is to vent during a team meeting without purposeful direction. The service team model recognizes this possibility. To ensure that every meeting considers solutions to the concerns and problems brought up by a team member, all teams are lead by a staff member who has received training as a facilitator of group communication and problem solving. The most important responsibility of a team facilitator is to organize the work of the team, which involves the following tasks:

- *Identifying students.* Helping the team prioritize the at-risk students for problem solving.
- *Developing summaries of information.* Presenting and sharing information on the student.
- *Problem solving.* Guiding the team through a problem-solving process by developing an action plan.
- *Monitoring progress.* Leading the team in monitoring the implementation of action plans and student progress toward a set of objectives.

I have found that this model helps to maintain a professional working environment, allowing each person to use his or her unique skills and to provide a renewed abundance of their energy to effectively problem solve. Unfortunately, not all teachers are convinced of the usefulness of meeting as a team which has set procedures for dealing with the problems that arise with students. For example, one of our team members was feeling that her time could be used more productively doing other things besides meeting weekly with the service team. When asked why she had stopped participating, she quickly responded, "I know my students and therefore could find solutions to their behavioral problems quicker than by spending a lot of time discussing them with a group of other people." Her frustration with the limited amount of time teachers have to accomplish many tasks was felt. But another colleague responded by repeating a quote he had recently read: "Some of us are more effective than others. But none of us is more effective than all of us." Another important aspect of teamwork is recognizing that helping all students gain the competencies and skills necessary to succeed is shared by all.

For a team to be effective in its work, all members must first want to be part of the team. Just as students learn more in cooperative groups, so do adults. We gain a great deal from interacting with our peers to accomplish a task. I tell students before introducing a cooperative group activity that, in the world of work, employers want people who can problem solve with others. Little is accomplished in isolation at school and in the real world of work. Most of what we do takes place in teams—or, at the least, with a teacher partner.

Accepting Diversity

Ideally, when forming teams, it is advisable to search for a balance in teaching styles and temperaments. But this is not always possible for a variety of reasons. One year I facilitated a service team which was made up of a very diverse group of adults. We had new and experienced teachers who seemed to share little or no common ground. One teacher had a reputation for using harsh words and sometimes harsher actions with his students. Another teacher was seen as a rescuer by taking on many of her students' responsibilities. We also had open-minded and well-balanced members. As team facilitator I realized that, for us to be effective, I needed to set a tone which respected others' (students' and adults') similarities and differences. Knowing myself, I could not afford to be narrow-minded or judgmental. My work was to consciously be the person I personally find most effective and enjoyable to be with. Being effective also included possessing traits that enhance the team effort—such as professionalism, an easy-going attitude, humor, open-mindedness, and flexibility.

During team time, when the talk became unprofessional, I reminded everyone of our purpose and redirected the focus without getting off balanced or becoming short-sighted. Fortunately, we eventually found our rhythm as a diverse group of professionals and consequently helped some difficult students to change their negative behavior cycles, as well as shared ideas on how to be more effective teachers of discipline.

Working together for the purpose of helping others involves reflection on how we communicate the values we teach to our students.

A diverse school community is not only acceptable but valued and respected. Diversity includes helping others feel that they are vital to the team process, however it manifests itself in school. Helping colleagues appreciate the power of teaming requires making sincere connections, and building confidence and trust in one another. In order for a team to function successfully from the beginning, all members must embrace the philosophy that

- Working in teams will make their teaching more effective
- Working in teams will improve the growth and development of students
- Working in teams will better meet both teachers' and students' needs

When this philosophy becomes a reality, teaming can then become a working aspect of how you operate as a school community. Having said this, it should be remembered that teaming development is ongoing. Regardless of the model your school embraces, the kinks in the program can be worked out over time, as the team members see a need for changes. New ideas can and should be implemented, adapted, or revised whenever the team feels it is necessary.

Changing Eleven Negative Behavior Cycles

This chapter looks at eleven common negative behavior cycles that will only change with well-matched and thoughtfully implemented interventions. The suggestions here can act as a quick reference guide when handling misbehaviors at school or at home. Each negative behavior is divided into the following three sections:

- *Behavior cycle.* The behavior cycles correspond with the explanations of the cycle of reinforcing attitudes and behaviors. These negative behavior or attitude cycles tend to reinforce themselves, as illustrated in Chapter 1. Identifying the behavior cycle gives the teacher a starting point from which educated decisions can be made. Identifying the student's behavior cycle is important because it identifies the characteristics of the behavior as well as the message the student gives to him or herself. These cycles should be illustrated and shared with the student.

- *Primary cause(s).* After identifying the behavior cycle, we define the primary causes of the behavior. Professional objectivity can be lost when we become overly involved in the student's actions. Understanding the possible reasons why a student acts the way he or she does can help us to maintain professional objectivity and is the next step toward using effective methods and interventions. We also understand that we can reduce misconduct by responding to its psychological origins.

Seeking attention is a primary cause for many misbehaviors. Why is this true? All people, young and older, want to be noticed. The technique of "catching them being good" focuses on giving positive attention to the student(s) when they are cooperating, amicably interacting with peers, sharing in a friendly manner, doing their work, and not whining or being petulant. A basic law in behavior management is that when an action is followed by a reward or positive reaction, that action is likely to be repeated.

But some teachers fall into the criticism trap or unknowingly give attention to their students for undesirable behaviors, and therefore teach their students the exact opposite of what they intended. When this occurs, instead of behaving well, the student acts up. The cycle looks like this: When exhibiting inner discipline, the teacher ignores the student. But as soon as the student begins to misbehave, he or she gets immediate attention from the teacher's lecture, reprimand, and so on. The operative word here is "attention." Students prefer their teachers' positive attention to their negative attention. But if the choice is between negative teacher or peer attention and no attention at all, they will usually choose the former. To a needy student, even negative attention is better than being ignored.

Teaching discipline can unwittingly become teaching misbehavior. Teachers can eliminate desirable behaviors from a student's school life by not giving attention to them. At the same time, they are busy training the student in undesirable behavior by rewarding it with negative attention. I once asked a student who was always in another teacher's classroom why I constantly saw him there. He responded by saying, "Ms. Pokes likes me and said if I get in trouble to come to her class." The established cycle became clear.

• *How to intervene.* To avoid mistakes that may support, instead of eliminate, negative behaviors, I offer several interventions. This section suggests possible quick actions to help students adjust their behaviors and ultimately change the way they see themselves. You can select the method(s) or technique(s) that best fit the student you are teaching.

1. THE CLASS BULLY

Bullies: A Case of Hidden Aggression

Sonny is repeatedly teased and called unpleasant names by Ben, who is bigger, more powerful, and has successfully persuaded other students to avoid Sonny as much as possible. As a result, Sonny is feeling angry, anxious, and isolated.

Bullying affects about five million elementary and middle school students in the United States. Some studies indicate that up to 70 percent of today's students have been victims of bullying. Unfortunately, the number of children being bullied by their peers does not seem to be decreasing. Creating safer schools should be a priority for all communities. "Bullying," according to noted expert Dan Olweus (n.d.), "poisons the educational environment and impacts the learning of every child." We need to address how to accomplish the goal of creating safer schools.

What causes this aggression toward others? Students—young and old—who exhibit bullying behavior are caught in a trap of hidden aggression. They believe that being powerful or strong means pushing others around. They have a distorted view of personal power and its effect on others. Students who bully have learned that they can get the much-desired attention of others by these actions. Students who are being bullied are robbed of their personal power. Bullying can leave them feeling helpless, anxious, inferior, afraid, and very angry.

Young Bullies

Bullies are raised in the home, but their victims are frequently created in the classroom. Older bullies usually learned this dysfunctional way of relating to others at a young age. Child bullies are always those who, as a result of initial discouragement, assume that they are "big" only when they can show their misuse of power. The child is often discouraged, which often leads to hidden aggression. For change to occur at a young age, we must recognize misbehavior as a mistaken approach brought about through discouragement. A simple and basic strategy when dealing with child bullies is first to avoid all discouraging remarks. What is needed is a lesson to be learned, not a punishment to be denied. When a child acts in an aggressive manner, the teacher communicates clearly that the behavior will not be tolerated but that the child will always be liked and cared for.

Helping Younger Students

Joseph wanted to play with Patty, who was looking at some pictures of flowers. When she wouldn't stop to play with him, he began threatening her with a pencil and harsh language. A common response would be to reprimand Joseph for his angry behavior and give him a directive to sit alone away from all the children. At that point, Joseph may shout out some words demonstrating his frustration and discouragement, feeling misunderstood and uncared for.

Once the bullying behavior began, the effective teacher quietly walked up to Joseph, took his hand, and said, "Joseph, I'm sorry you feel so angry. Since you don't feel like playing in a nice way with Patty, you can come and sit with me." Of course, this makes it necessary for the teacher to spend some time with Joseph until he has regained his self-control. But such an intervention can "teach" Joseph that he may play with Patty again if he is willing to talk in a nonaggressive manner. If the teacher can accept Joseph by exhibiting an attitude of sincere caring for him, even though his behavior is unfriendly, she offers encouragement without condoning his misbehavior. The teacher has allowed Joseph to take responsibility for his behavior and has provided a necessary opportunity for him to reflect on the natural consequences of bullying. When the teacher suggests that he can play with Patty again when "he is ready," she expresses her faith in his ability to reconsider his misuse or abuse of his power and to play appropriately at a later time.

For change to occur, a child bully must be given three messages:

1. We understand that bullying is a cover for your hidden anger.

2. Aggressive behavior will never be tolerated but you'll always be cared for.

3. We have faith in your ability to cope with and learn from adversity.

It is equally important that the child who is being bullied understands what it means to stick up for him or herself. Kaufman (in Kaufman, Raphael, & Espeland, 1999) advises telling students that sticking up for oneself means knowing

- Who you are and what you stand for, and being true to yourself
- How to speak up for yourself, and doing so when it's the right thing to do (sometimes it isn't)
- That there's always someone on your side—you (p. 3)

Older Bullies

We have found that boys and girls are defined in different ways through media and society's norms. Society teaches that it is okay for boys, but not girls, to have mean and aggressive feelings. Although girls feel the same aggressive emotions as boys, they learn to channel these feelings into acceptable forms. In place of direct physical and verbal behavior, girls may use silence, exclusion, or rumors whereas boys tend to be loud,

Bullying

aggressive, and directly confrontational. Much of the behavior exhibited by girls is too subtle to be noticed by teachers and parents. In her book *Odd Girl Out: The Hidden Culture of Aggression in Girls,* Rachel Simmons (2003) describes three types of aggressive behavior in girls:

1. The first type uses others as pawns to indirectly hurt someone, such as by spreading a rumor.

2. The second type tries to damage self-esteem or status within a group.

3. The third type uses friendship as a weapon.

Boys tend to exhibit some similar as well as clearly different types of aggressive behavior:

1. The first type abuses others with aggressive talk or physical threats.

2. The second type tries to damage self-esteem by using undermining comments.

3. The third type takes advantage of someone's insecurities by using them for personal gain.

Why do girls and boys often try to stay friends with others who treat them cruelly? And why do respectful students follow a leader into aggressive acts? In both cases, the reason—especially with girls—is the fear of solitude, which can be overpowering. And with boys the fear of not being cool and seen as potentially aggressive can be disabling. Older students often define themselves through connections with others, so being alone can be seen as losing your identity. Self-determination begins with group identity and eventually returns to individual awareness. Older students may therefore avoid being alone, even if it means staying in abusive friendships or abusing others. A boy seeking attention may do anything to show his power over others. A girl seeking popularity may do anything to show her loyalty to the "right" people.

Helping Middle and High School Students

All schools should introduce anti-bullying messages that include the subtle behaviors of girls as well as the shoving and physical threats most commonly used by boys. Behaviors associated with bullying should be clearly defined and rules enforced. As I explained, parents and teachers should begin communicating with their children from early childhood. Establishing a connection with the potential bully as well as the victim during the time when you are the central figure in the child's life is very important. If you continue this connection as they get older, children will learn to trust adults and be more likely to come to you for guidance.

Children who are bullied need to understand that it is not their fault and that no one ever deserves to be bullied. Sometimes children may confuse teasing with bullying. Teasing can be fun, but bullying is always hurtful. Teachers can discuss bullying behavior in class. Behaviors such as hitting, pushing, name calling, putting others down, excluding, and threatening all constitute bullying behaviors. Let students know that

1. When being bullied, they should not react in a fearful manner. They need to stand up straight, look at the bully, and say in an assertive voice, "Leave me alone!" Bullies don't bully those who stick up for themselves.

2. They should tell their parents. If the bullying is happening at school, they need to tell a teacher. Because bullies do most of their bullying when adults are not around, teachers are usually not aware of the bullying unless they are told.

3. If a bully is bothering them, they need to walk away—if possible, toward their friends or other students they know. The bully will

most likely stay away from the large group and thus can't bother the student.

The Colorado Anti-Bullying Project for students in elementary school uses the acronym STAMP to help students understand how they can avoid being bullied:

Stay away from bullies.

Tell someone.

Avoid bad situations.

Make friends.

Project confidence.

Not all teachers agree on the subject of bullying and what—if anything—should be done about it. But we can all agree that students who exhibit bullying behavior are caught in a trap of hidden aggression.

Projecting Confidence

One of the most unpleasant and stressful problems for teachers is maintaining a positive classroom climate when the class contains a student who is hostile toward others. We understand that a teacher will never win a test of wills with a student who exhibits bullying behavior. However, we do not want to ignore this behavior because there is always a victim involved. When it comes to bullying behavior, ignorance is not bliss.

Behavior Cycle

The class bully is a case of hidden aggression or anger at something or someone. The student sees himself as someone who verbally or physically pushes other around. They find a "victim" and become verbally or physically aggressive.

> The bully's self-message is "I can't control my hidden aggression when I'm angry."

Primary Causes

The class bully gets attention from peers and adults, which consequently creates a feeling of control and personal power. The student may understand that hurting others is wrong, but will use this abuse of power to cover up his or her low self-esteem.

How to Intervene

1. Build a relationship with the bully. This student is most likely missing this important connection with a healthy, successful adult. Become friendly by deliberately not mirroring the aggressive behavior the student exhibits toward others. Be gentle rather than tough. Give the bully nothing to fight against.

2. Show the student the bullying cycle in which he or she is caught up and address the possible reasons for their insecurity. Openly discussing the possible causes of low self-esteem, such as negative experiences at home and school, can help redirect energies constructively.

3. With the student present, invite a parent and other concerned adults to a private conference to discuss the problem. Ensure the student clearly understands that bullying behavior will not be tolerated—giving the message that you respect all people in the school community.

4. Explain what things can be done to change the negative behavior cycle, such as working with a peer who will be an appropriate role model, removing the student if the bulling behavior begins, and emphasizing individual success or progress rather than "beating" other students. Praise the student when you catch him or her in respectful interactions. Give the student opportunities for personal success.

Building Character

When we look at prevention and proactive means of addressing the problem of bullying behavior in our schools, it becomes apparent that a student's belief system and self-esteem play a large part in this process. Character building addresses the cause of many of the problems inherent in bullying behavior. We recognize that all children need a set of core beliefs that will guide their behavior in school and in the community.

Many school districts across the country increasingly see the importance of character education as a link to decreasing misbehavior in schools. In Pittsburgh, Pennsylvania, schools recently launched the Your Environment Education Program, which is designed to help children succeed by improving their behavior, both in and out of school. Dale Frederick, District Superintendent of Schools in Pittsburgh, Pennsylvania, feels that "academics is the cornerstone of education, but character is the building block of life." In several of their elementary schools, teachers typically spend time each day discussing the word of the week—such as "respect," "trust," "kindness," "courage," or "honesty"—with students. Stories that illustrate real-life implications of the highlighted trait are also shared and then discussed among the students. Each week a new word becomes the focus of classroom activities and discussions. The foundations of self-discipline are also being taught.

Including families as partners in the character-building process is also a large part of a character-building program, as is getting the community to advertise and support the school's efforts. For example, the Springfield, Massachusetts, schools are actively involved with a communitywide program called Step Up Springfield. This initiative addresses the social, behavioral, and academic needs of all the students. With the help from celebrities such as Bill Cosby, parents, teachers, and businesses work together for the purpose of raising behavioral and academic expectations of all students by bringing attention to the issues and by supporting teachers and parents in their work with children. These initiatives are just a few examples of what some communities are doing to build character among their student population, therefore increasing the safety within their schools.

Most schools in which I've taught take bullying seriously. But teachers are often divided in their views on the subject of bullying, character building, and what—if anything—should be done about this problem. Some believe it is part of the growing-up process in any school and should not be blown out of proportion. Others think the issue is of enormous importance and stress that preventing bullying behavior is essential. Some teachers feel that bullying can be stopped by punitive means; some believe that you can reason with bullies, get them to like you, and therefore change their behavior. Other teachers think you can't reason with bullies because they are far too emotionally disturbed and beyond rational thinking. Most feel that victims can be taught to stand up for themselves or avoid bullies, while others think nothing will work.

2. THE CLASS CLOWN

Behavior Cycle

Most classrooms have a "class clown," but few teachers seem to understand how to help this student change the behavior without creating a mini-war between them and the student. I understand this behavior well because there was a time in elementary school when I felt the need to play this role. The class clown disrupts the class with comments meant to be humorous. This student wants to be in the spotlight but usually doesn't know when to stop.

> The class clown's self-message is "I need to make jokes to be noticed."

This student will make comments that are often "wisecracks" and elicit laughter from peers. The teacher will usually ask the student to control such comments, which will usually be answered by another wisecrack. The teacher then either reprimands the student or asks him or her to leave.

Primary Causes

It's evident that this student desires attention and clowning is the way to get it. But the cause may also include a need to be liked by peers and teachers, and clowning comes naturally to the student who may have a limited repertoire of interpersonal skills.

How to Intervene

1. Occasionally enjoy the class clown's humor along with your students, and a relationship with the joker will be more easily formed. The problem with the class clown is not knowing when to stop. Working out a signal that is not so revealing or obvious to others can be helpful (e.g., touching your ear, or laying a finger over closed lips). Avoid bringing the class's attention to the problem.

2. In private, illustrate the negative behavior cycle and explain how humor can be a good thing if used at the correct time with the right people. Demonstrate how the student may be losing respect from others by allowing him or herself to always be laughed at.

3. At appropriate times and places, allow this student a chance to entertain others—something class clowns love to do. The key is enabling the student to express a strength without losing self-respect and maturity. Explain these traits and the importance of maturity and not losing self-respect with their peers.

3. THE INTERRUPTER

Behavior Cycle

When a student occasionally interrupts the teacher, this behavior is normal and should be expected. However, "the interrupter" will consistently try to take the class's attention and discussion off the topic with questions,

> The interrupter's self-message is "I need to blurt out answers to gain attention from others."

opinions, or comments. This student will blurt out answers and make comments without being called on. Often, angry responses by the teacher or peers have only a temporary effect.

Primary Causes

The student who interrupts others may see this behavior as the only way he or she can gain status with peers. Getting desired attention from the teacher and peers is also a cause of this misbehavior.

How to Intervene

1. Do not give the student attention by stopping teaching and giving a reprimand. Staying calm and continuing the lesson gives the message that the behavior will not interrupt the momentum of the class. If the behavior continues, develop hand signals which tell the student to either stop immediately and/or move to the time out area.

2. When the student interrupts, write his or her name on the chalkboard while continuing your teaching. If the interrupting continues, put a check mark after the student's name. If the student doesn't interrupt after five minutes, erase a check. Continue this procedure every five minutes until checks and the name are erased. A consequence can be attached to checks if there are still checks not erased by the end of the class.

3. Have a private conference with the student and illustrate the cycle in which he or she is caught. Next, in a firm voice, explain that the disrupting of the learning process in class will not be tolerated. Make sure the student understands you are very serious. Explain that you will give a

warning to stop and then there will be a swift consequence which may include going to the "teacher buddy" room for the remainder of the class.

4. THE DISORGANIZED STUDENT

Behavior Cycle

> The disorganized student's self-message is "I continue to lose things and forget to do assignments. I can't be organized."

The disorganized student's notebook is either full of crumpled papers dating back to the beginning of the year, or empty. The student usually doesn't write assignments down or writes them on a piece of paper and then forgets where it is. This disorganization extends to schoolwork, materials, school locker, homework, and life itself.

Primary Causes

The student who is continually disorganized is usually feeling incapable of doing the work he or she has been given. Many students who also have a learning disability are disorganized and have learned to use it as a cover for their future failures.

How to Intervene

1. Have the student question any directions, explanations, and instructions he or she does not understand. Simplify the steps in completing an assignment.

2. Assign a peer to accompany the student to specified activities in order to make certain the student has the necessary materials, assignments, books, and so on.

3. Provide the student with an assignment book and an organizational checklist (e.g., specific directions, routines, format for tasks, time units) that is checked at the end of the day by a teacher or paraeducator. The parents are asked to check the book at night and sign it, indicating that the student has completed the work.

4. Make certain that work not completed because necessary materials were not brought to the specified activity is completed during recreational time or break time.

5. Avoid putting too much pressure on the student. This can be accomplished by establishing a one-on-one relationship that creates a situation in which the student will want to follow your model for being organized/prepared for specified activities.

5. THE OVERLY SENSITIVE STUDENT

Behavior Cycle

The overly sensitive student may respond inappropriately to friendly joking or teasing by withdrawing or verbally attacking others. They sometimes can seem to be afraid of interacting with people—both students and adults—out of a fear being emotionally hurt.

> The overly sensitive student's self-message is "I continue to be made fun of. I'm not likable."

Primary Causes

The primary cause of this behavior is a lack of self-confidence. The overly sensitive student often reacts by being alone, and this takes a certain amount of inner strength. The teacher should draw on this inner boldness to help change the negative reinforcing cycle.

How to Intervene

1. Don't assume that something is wrong with the student who is overly sensitive. The goal is not to protect or change this student but to create opportunities for the overly sensitive student to engage in interactions that are healthy and that contribute to the class.

2. Teach the student appropriate ways in which to respond to friendly teasing (e.g., laugh, joke in return). I have found it helpful to role-play situations with the student and then give immediate feedback. Other students can be involved in the role-playing.

3. Gently urge the student to participate, but do not force the student to interact with others with whom she or he is not comfortable. Encourage others to compliment the student.

4. Point out to the student, when she or he is being teased in a friendly way, that no harm is meant. Explain that friendly joking is a positive means by which people demonstrate that they like other people and enjoy their company. Model friendly joking with all students. Reinforce the overly sensitive student for responding appropriately to friendly teasing (e.g., praise, handshake, smile).

6. THE TEASER

Behavior Cycle

This student makes remarks at the expense of others. It is not uncommon for an older sibling to tease a younger brother or sister, or for boys to tease girls. The teaser exhibits this behavior repeatedly to someone of subordinate rank, supposedly in the spirit of having fun—however, nobody is laughing. The teaser may expect the other person to respond good-naturedly, and maybe even to enjoy the interaction.

> The teaser's self-message is "I'm a funny person who needs to tease others to be liked."

Primary Causes

The primary cause of this behavior is a lack of self-confidence and a need for attention. The teaser can lack acquired social skills and possibly needs quick feedback and monitoring. Often this behavior stems from a form of defense against others getting too close. For example, "If I tease, people will have a hard time getting to know who I really am." The teaser doesn't think much of him or herself.

How to Intervene

1.   Catch the student engaging in friendly and positive interpersonal behaviors. Set up a positive reward system which deals only with the action of teasing, not the student's feelings. The student may not be able to change feelings of being sad, fearful, or angry, but can stop teasing others. The positive reward system should be based on actions and consequences. List the actions you approve of, the actions you want to see less of, and those you want to see more of (e.g., interacting in a friendly, respectful manner). Give positive attention to desirable behavior and use thinking time when teasing occurs.

2.   Hold a private conference with the student and parent(s) to determine why he or she teases others. Explain that teasing always has a victim and it will not be tolerated. Sometimes the teaser does not fully realize the hurt caused by teasing. Make it clear to the student that teasing others can hurt as much as if he or she physically hit them.

3.   Discuss with the student ways he or she could deal with unpleasant experiences which would typically cause teasing (e.g., talk to the teacher or counselor, take a break in a quiet area of the school).

7. THE PROPERTY DESTROYER

Behavior Cycle

The student who destroys property is found ripping pages in books, marking up desks and walls, and destroying school or other students' property.

Primary Causes

The primary cause of this behavior is seeded in anger and revenge. This student has a need to show his or her hostility by instilling fear in people and destroying things. This student is usually at risk of failing.

> The property destroyer's self-message is "I need to break rules and destroy things."

How to Intervene

1. Allow for logical consequences to occur as the result of the student's inability to appropriately care for and handle others' property. For example, if a book is destroyed, it needs to be replaced; if a desk is marked, it needs to be washed. Consequences should be given in a professional manner without lecture or severe reprimand.

2. Teach the student appropriate care and handling of others' property (e.g., keeping books free of marks and tears). Teach how to conserve rather than waste materials.

3. Involve parents in helping the student to understand appropriate ways to deal with anger and frustration rather than destroying others' property. Make the necessary adjustments in the environment to prevent the student from experiencing stress, frustration, anger, and so on as much as possible. Parents should also be partners in any contract agreed upon for giving the student full responsibility for his or her behavior.

8. THE FIGHTER

Behavior Cycle

The student who is continually involved in physical aggression and fights with other students has a fighting mentality—a mental attitude that supports harming others before he or she gets hurt. This student sees no other options for dealing with problems.

> The fighter's self-message is "I am the strongest when I fight."

Primary Causes

The primary cause of this behavior is a need for attention from adults and peers. Some fighters will only begin a physical confrontation if a teacher is in view. Others will wait until after school or during times when the teacher is not in sight, such as during recess. Poor self-esteem includes feeling powerless. This student sees the strongest as having the most manipulative power.

How to Intervene

1.   Listen to what the student has to say when he or she feels the need to fight. Students who continually fight because they need to demonstrate "power" over others—either physically or through psychological manipulation, as in bullying—are often making up for the lack of a sense of personal power. Explain to the student that real power is exercised by controlling one's body and emotions, and by making wise decisions. Having a sense of power is not the same as "being powerful." People and countries arm themselves when they feel insecure, not when they are confident about their own power.

2.   Establish goals for the fighter that will help to reinforce acceptable in-school behavior. Teach this student problem-solving skills: (a) identify the problem; (b) identify the goals; (c) develop strategies; (d) develop a plan of action; and (e) carry out the plan.

3.   Use group exercises for enhancing social skills and self-esteem (Khalsa, 1999) as a resource for helping these students to gain the understanding, practice, and experience needed for controlling aggressive behavior.

4.   When two students need help changing a cycle of fighting each other, offer a positive reinforcement for not fighting. For example, "I know both of you don't get along but the fighting must stop. Here are your choices. You can continue fighting and deal with the consequences of being sent to the office, having your parents called, and possibly being suspended from school. The other option is not fighting. If we talk next Friday and you did not fight, I will reward both of you for your efforts in controlling yourselves [e.g., snack at lunch, extra computer time, art]." I've used this intervention numerous times and noticed how two students who were once adversaries can become partners.

5.   Maintain maximum supervision of the student and gradually decrease supervision over time as the student demonstrates appropriate behavior.

9. THE STUDENT WHO FEELS STUPID

Behavior Cycle

The student who claims "I can't do this" and "I'm stupid" is caught in a cycle of negative reinforcing attitudes. This student may or may not have a learning disability but often finds school work overwhelming.

Primary Causes

The primary cause of this behavior is a lack of self-confidence due to a history of failure and absence of self-knowledge. For these students, saying "I'm stupid" has become a means of excusing themselves from participating in the classroom.

> The student who feels stupid's self-message is "I can't do this. I must be stupid."

How to Intervene

1. Determine whether the student is playing stupid or feeling stupid. If he or she is playing stupid, treat it as a discipline problem. If the student is feeling stupid, approach it as a poor self-concept problem. For example, affirm success—no matter how small, or in what area of life—then build the student's confidence by recognizing and appreciating successes. Provide opportunities for the student to practice and demonstrate things he or she can do particularly well.

2. Give the "stupid test." For someone to change, they first need to be aware of where they are. When a student says, "I'm stupid or dumb," respond in this manner: "Well, maybe you are stupid. Can I give you the 'stupid test'?" I've never met a student who said no. "If I wanted you to measure the height of this building, would you climb out the window and on to the roof with a yard stick and jump off?" When the student responds, "No!" you then say, "Well, you are not stupid. But if you decided to skip school, that would be . . . right, stupid. If you took drugs, that would be . . . If you punched someone for calling you a name, that would be . . . stupid. But if you are having a hard time reading a word, or understanding how to solve a math problem, that may mean you need some extra time or a different instruction."

3. Review the student's work privately with him or her. If effort is being made, make allowances for errors. Respect the student's present level of competence by appreciating what can be done, and praise him or her for it.

10. THE NERVOUS STUDENT

Behavior Cycle

The student who engages in nervous habits such as picking at their face or excessive biting of nails usually receives negative feedback from adults and peers.

> The nervous student's self-message is "I can't control myself."

Primary Causes

The primary cause of this behavior is a lack of self-awareness and self-confidence due to a history of engaging in nervous habits. This student's self-esteem is low due to the negative feedback often heard from other adults and peers.

How to Intervene

1. Reduce situations which may contribute to nervous behavior (e.g., testing situations, timed activities, competition).

2. Discuss the nervous habit in private (e.g., chewing on pencil, biting nails). Giving the student information about him or herself will increase self-awareness and improve the ability to control a potentially unconscious habit. Recognize the effects of the nervous habit and explore compensatory interventions which can prevent the negative results of the behavior (e.g., putting hand in sleeve to prevent picking pimples on face).

3. Intervene early when the student begins to engage in nervous habits in order to prevent more serious problems from occurring and to increase awareness.

4. Reinforce the student for demonstrating appropriate behavior—for example, "I noticed your face is clearing up. Looks good."

11. THE STUDENT WHO MAKES SEXUAL OVERTONES

Behavior Cycle

> The self-message of the student who makes sexual overtones is "I need to act sexual to get attention."

The student who engages in behavior with sexual overtones tries to gratify all sensual desires immediately and crudely. They may make sexual comments, or touch the opposite sex by hugging, walking, and/or talking too close. This student is criticism avoidant and makes excuses for such inappropriate behavior.

Primary Causes

The primary cause of this behavior is a need for attention and poor role models. Students who have responsible adult models on whom they can rely on and whom they respect, and who have been exposed to understandable and consistent guidelines for their behavior will be able to determine right from wrong most the time.

How to Intervene

1.   Remember that in school you are a primary model for your students. Exemplify principles of right conduct in your own behavior. Be an example of acting according to your beliefs. This student will be observing closely.

2.   Counsel the student privately. Explain (a) what the student is doing wrong (e.g., making sexual references, touching others, making gestures) and (b) what the student should be doing (e.g., following rules, respecting others, attending to responsibilities). Be careful not to fall into a criticism trap by inadvertently reinforcing the student for demonstrating sexually related behaviors (e.g., attending to the student only when sexually related behaviors are observed, demonstrating shock).

3.   Confer with other teachers, the school counselor, administrators, parent(s), and student. Make it clear that the sexually related comments and behavior are not acceptable in school—and stress that if the behavior continues, the student will be removed.

4.   Avoid asking the student why they behave in this manner. "Why" is not the issue and does not need to be debated. What the student is *doing* is the issue here.

5.   Maintain visibility to and from the student. The teacher should be able to see the student and the student should be able to see the teacher, making eye contact possible at all times.

Understanding Diverse Students and Difficult Circumstances

WORKING WITH STUDENTS AND FAMILIES WHO ARE DISADVANTAGED

I enjoy working in an urban school district that offers a clear challenge and diversity among its staff and students that may not be an inherent part of many of our suburban schools. But when I began teaching in one of this district's several middle schools, it was surprising to find out that 80 percent of the students were eligible for free school lunches—which meant that these students came from families living in poverty. The implications of this quickly became apparent. I soon realized that, after growing up and teaching in suburban schools, my approach toward teaching discipline to students from backgrounds of poverty had to change in order for me to be effective.

Our middle school principal would share ongoing research which showed that students who are impoverished can achieve high standards and consequently should be held to high academic and behavioral expectations. Mrs. Johnson would remind us that "it is not right to think that one group of students can't perform because of their home life or how much money their parents have or don't have." One study that supported this mind-set came from Beuleah Heights Elementary School in Pueblo,

Colorado (reported on the Internet in 2002), where 100 percent of Hispanic third graders from needy homes scored at the proficient level or higher on their standardized tests. This was attributed to well-trained and experienced teachers who maintained high expectations of all their students. Academically, this made sense. However, I have found that some approaches used for teaching discipline differ for students who come from middle-class homes versus students from disadvantaged areas.

We need to alter the way we teach appropriate behaviors necessary for success in the school community when teaching students from lower socioeconomic status groups. Many of the behaviors displayed in school by students who are poor have helped them to survive outside of school. For example, students of poverty need to know how to physically defend themselves, otherwise they will be in danger on the streets. But if they are limited only to this method of solving problems, they will never be successful in school.

The majority of needy students come from sole-parent homes which are governed by the mother or other female relatives. In matriarchal family systems of poverty, the mother will be the judge and jury. She dispenses punishment and gives forgiveness. When all is forgiven, life returns to the way it was before the incident occurred. Consequently, children become accustomed to being told what to do, how to do it, and what will happen if it is not done. This external evaluative voice often creates a dependency on parental guidance. Teachers who make a lot of demands and use harsh words and sometimes harsher actions often fail to make a positive impact on these students. There is a psychological as well as logical reason why this is often true.

Many of our students from poverty tend to become "parentified." This is due to circumstances that create a need for them to parent themselves as well as their siblings. It was initially startling for me to discover the high percentage of students in my middle school who were expected to take care of their younger brothers and sisters, and essentially become the parent in their household. Taking on this parental role at such an early age has some logical consequences.

Different Voices

Gestalt therapy was given new impetus and direction in the 1970s by Dr. Frederick Perls (1983). The aim of Gestalt therapy is to help a person become "whole" by becoming aware of fractured aspects of their personality. In structural analysis, which is the study of individual personality, each person is seen as having three ego states which are separate and distinct sources of behavior: the child ego state, the parent ego state, and the adult ego state. Today, one way we can help our students and teachers to label three internal voices which guide behavior and actions is by referring to them as the "child" voice, the "parent" voice, and the "adult" voice.

The internal child voice contains all the impulses that come naturally to an infant. As those of us who have raised our own children or who work in the primary grades understand, the child voice can be defensive, emotional, and whining. "It's not my fault," "I'm mad because of you," "I hate you." These statements are not uncommon from children who have created a problem that needs to be addressed. The child voice can also be lighthearted, playful, curious, and exploratory in nature.

The internal parent voice tends to be authoritative, evaluative, critical, and dependent on punishments and threats. It is a trap that some adults fall into. "You should do that and should not do this" are common words from the parent voice. A high school student once told me in a humorous way that at times he felt "should upon" by his teachers and parents. The parent voice can also be one of support and nurturance. In many cultures, the parent voice will try to create guilt and shame for misbehavior. This voice often fluctuates in and out of these phases due to external conflict and circumstances.

Not unlike the other voices, the internal adult voice does not necessarily relate to the person's age. It is organized, reality based, adaptable, assertive, open, and maintains a win-win attitude. Rational thinking and effective problem solving come from the adult voice. "Let's see, what are some of our choices?" "How can we deal with this situation without creating a bigger problem?" Statements such as these create a situation where people want to listen and contribute without the fear of threats or annoyance from immature behavior.

Students and teachers often respond to a specific event in different ways, depending on the internal voice they choose or have a habit of listening to. Sometimes these voices are in concert, sometimes they are in conflict. Here are a few examples.

SCENARIOS FOR RESPONDING TO EVENTS: INTERNAL VOICES

Scenario: The teacher brings in a piece of modern art.

Parent Voice: *What is that supposed to be?*

Adult Voice: *That's interesting. It reminds me of a Picasso.*

Child Voice: *Ooh, what nice colors!*

Scenario: The teacher explains the consequence for late homework.

Parent Voice: *Mr. Khalsa doesn't know how to teach.*

Adult Voice: *I have to make sure I get my homework in on time.*

Child Voice: *That's not fair. I can't pass this class.*

It has been Payne's (1996) observation that individuals who have become their own parent quite young do not have an internal adult voice. They have a child voice and a parent voice, but not an adult voice. It has been my observation that some teachers have a tendency to speak to their students primarily in a parent voice, especially when disciplining. Payne also points out that, to the students who are already functioning as a parent, this is unbearable—and almost immediately the incident escalates beyond the original event or comment.

The Ability to Negotiate

The adult voice is nonthreatening as well as assertive. It helps people solve problems by exploring alternatives while allowing them to make their own decisions. Because students who are economically disadvantaged have little or no practice with negotiating skills, directly teaching students to use their adult voice when dealing with problem situations is essential. In families from impoverished backgrounds, daily events are usually based around basic survival needs, which leaves little room for looking at options or negotiating skills. For example, if there are four people, four potatoes and leftover spaghetti for dinner, the distribution of the food is already determined. The amount of leftover spaghetti will be limited so the discussion will be limited as well. Conversely, in a typical middle-class household, the discussion over dinner may include how many potatoes each person would like with which vegetables, condiments, dessert, and so on. Helping students to use negotiating skills requires teaching and practicing them—just as with any new skill. The handout used in Lesson Box 6.1 details some steps for negotiation. The lesson box, which deals with interpersonal negotiation, may assist in teaching students to use the adult voice.

A parent showed up unannounced for a meeting concerning her son's behavior. Because the teachers were unable to leave their classrooms, I was asked by the guidance counselor to meet with her. She began by saying, "I'd like teachers to treat me and my child with the same respect they want themselves. I never hear from you until the problem with my son is so serious that it would take a miracle from God to fix it." I let her vent for a few more minutes and then asked her for some specifics. She said, "Like last year when Orlando stopped doing his social studies homework. The teacher couldn't be bothered to inform me of the fact until the week before report cards came out. How's my kid supposed to make up eleven assignments in one week?" I then asked why she thought the teacher did not contact her earlier in the semester. She said, "Well, we didn't have a phone for a while and the teacher never sent home a note or maybe my son never gave it to me. I don't know why."

This incident led me to reflect on the importance of staying in touch with parents even if they can't afford a phone. It was evident that what this mother wanted was respect and support. Some families, especially those from backgrounds of poverty, need support to keep up with their responsibilities. But often they are reluctant to come into school because the assumption is that the lack of income equates with a lack of intelligence. Many parents from poverty seem to have a school phobia. They dislike coming to conferences because bad memories of their own school days come flooding back. Poor parents are also offended when spoken to in a parent voice by their child's teacher. They often feel scolded or spoken to in a manner that instills guilt rather than hope.

Building partnerships with all families requires a mutual understanding that both teachers and parents have remarkably similar needs which include

- Appreciation, information, and understanding from one another
- Efforts acknowledged by both parent and teacher
- Respect for one another's jobs
- A need to work together and support each other so both can give the best to the student

A warm, welcoming attitude is probably the best antidote to their anxieties. I suggest a closed door when conferencing as well. It signals respect for the private time they spend with you. Setting a tone which

(Text continues on page 130)

Lesson Box 6.1 A Lesson for Interpersonal Negotiation

Materials

News print or chalkboard, markers, "Steps for Negotiation" (Activity Sheet 6.1), "Negotiation Role-Plays" (Activity Sheet 6.2)

Setting the Stage

- Write the word "negotiation" on the board and ask students for a definition. Explain that, in negotiation, the students or students and teacher in conflict "talk things out."
- Negotiation is a process in which two or more people talk to each other in order to solve a problem and reach an agreement.

Objective

Students will

- Learn a problem-solving process
- Understand skills essential for effective negotiation
- Practice negotiating

Purpose

- To increase effective communication/dialogue
- To manage and resolve conflicts

Background Information

- Students need an understanding of how to role-play.
- It is important to understand the meaning of negotiation as an alternative to aggression.

Instructions

1. Explain to the students that in this lesson they are going to learn that all of us negotiate something every day. Some of us have more opportunities to do so and therefore are better at it than others. Negotiation is a set of skills that can be improved by practice.

2. Make a web chart on the chalkboard with the word "basketball" in the center circle. Ask students to think of the skills, knowledge, and personal qualities needed to be a good basketball player. Illustrate answers on the web for the class to see.

3. Give the "Steps for Negotiation" handout to each student to read silently as you read aloud. Make another web on the board and ask students to fill in the skills necessary for effective negotiation.

4. Ask students to form groups of three. Each triad chooses two role-plays from the "Negotiation Role-Plays" handout, or they could create their own conflict situation. In each role-play, two students will play two people in conflict and try to negotiate a solution using the "Steps for Negotiation" handout as a guide. The third student will act as an observer. The observer will give feedback to the role-players on their use of effective communication skills.

5. Explain that these role-plays will take no longer than five minutes each. After each role-play, allow three minutes for the observers to give their feedback.

Summary

After the activity, discuss what observers noticed students doing that helped them negotiate effectively? Ask whether this process is more effective than fighting. If so, why or why not?

Activity Sheet 6.1   Steps for Negotiation

Step 1: See That There's a Conflict and Agree to Solve It

This first step cannot happen when both people are still angry and upset. It is always best to wait until your emotions have cooled down and you are ready to talk with rather than at each other. Sometimes this might mean walking away and returning when both of you are ready to start the negotiation process.

Step 2: Define the Problem and Take Turns Sharing Points of View

- Take turns sharing what you each think the problem is and how you feel by using "I" messages. One of you talks while the other listens. "I get angry when you . . ."
- Check to see whether you understand what the other student is saying and feeling.
- Try to agree on what caused the problem.

Step 3: Discuss Solutions

List all ideas and possible solutions to the problem. How could each of you make some changes to help come to an agreement? For example, ask questions such as "What if you . . . ?" "Could we . . . ?" "If I . . . will you . . . ?"

Step 4: Evaluate Solutions

Which solutions are most realistic and responsible? Solutions that will not work should be discarded, then the focus shifted to those that can work.

Step 5: Choose and Implement Your Solution

Does the solution satisfy both of you? If the answer is yes, then agree on the solution and feel good about being able to solve a problem in a mature way. Set a time to evaluate how your plan worked.

Activity Sheet 6.2 Negotiation Role-Plays

Role-Play 1

Older Sibling: You are concerned that if you tell your mother about a party you want to attend she won't let you go. You confided to your younger sibling that you were thinking of going to the party and not telling your mother about it. You made your sibling promise not to tell your mother. When you came home from school the following day, your mother announced that you were grounded for even thinking of lying to her.

Younger Sibling: You are asked by your mother whether you know anything about a party that your sister wants to attend this weekend. You feel pressure to tell the truth. You never asked your sibling to confide in you about this, and you are upset that you have been put in this situation.

Role-Play 2

Student: You notice that your best friend has been ignoring you for no apparent reason. In the hallway, you overhear another student saying that your best friend thinks you're a liar and can't be trusted. You're really upset and confront your best friend about what you heard.

Best Friend: You decide to start making friends with some other students because you think your best friend has been spreading rumors about you and someone else you don't even hang out with. Because you're not sure whether the rumors are true, you decide to just stop hanging around with your best friend until you find out the truth.

Role-Play 3

Student: Your family has been dealing with a lot of problems. You're going to be moving to another apartment and your brother recently got into trouble with the police. You're behind in your assignments, you haven't begun to do your poetry book that is due next week, and you've got a cold that won't go away. You want to work out a schedule to complete your assignments and want to turn in your poetry book a week late so that you can do a good job.

Teacher: You have a homework policy that all students know and agreed to at the beginning of the year. Late homework is worth half of the points. You're not aware of the student's family problems but want all your students to do a good job on their projects. You want to be fair, but changing deadlines concerns you because it may upset other students as well as leaving more time for procrastination.

A Common Commitment to Progress

(Text continued from page 125)

highlights each student's strengths and efforts is an effective strategy for creating the mutual trust necessary for dealing with the problems at hand. Every conference, regardless how long or short, in person or by phone, should end with a prevailing feeling of being on the same team, bound together by a common commitment to the student's progress and well-being.

Teaching Students Who Are Disadvantaged: Empathetic Straight Talk

Payne (1996) suggests that students need to have at least two sets of behaviors from which to choose—one set for the streets and one set for school or work. The use of empathetic straight talk is another technique to help some students from impoverished neighborhoods differentiate between these two behaviors. The following conversation takes place in the classroom.

Student: *This is bullshit! I didn't take her book.*

Teacher: *Cameron, let's talk outside the classroom for a moment. Do you use the same rules when I see you playing basketball and football?*

Student: *No. Why?*

Teacher: *You're right. Otherwise you would create so many penalties that your team would lose or you would be kicked out of the game. The same is true for school. Every rule is there to help you be successful at what you are doing and where you are. I know you like that word, "B. S" On the street it can be a good word. In school it's not acceptable language. Two different places, two different rules. I don't know if you took her book but by swearing you'll only get into more trouble. Do you understand my point?*

Student: *Yeah. But I still didn't take her book.*

Teacher: *Okay. Now that I can hear what you're saying, we'll deal with this after class.*

This example of empathetic straight talk left the student with an important lesson to reflect upon. The teacher made an attempt to empathize with the student's mind-set and worldview. When educating students from poverty, we need to be careful about seeing their behavior through our own colored glasses. The key to building relationships is to understand another's point of view and experiences. The teacher in this dialogue was not condoning a misperception or misbehavior, but communicating an understanding of it so that effective action could follow. With students from poverty, I recommend that this straight talk should include the opposing rules of the street and school, and then a discussion of which rules will make them be successful in their school community.

My colleague, Orlander Worthy, once said, "When we want our children to learn how to drive, we teach them. When we want them to learn to read, we teach them. When they misbehave, we react to them when teaching is what's called for." There are certain lessons a student from poverty should learn in order to be successful in school and at work. But before these lessons can be taught, I recommend the following:

- Look at your own biases. Recognize poverty as a diversity issue. Not unlike differences in race, gender, and learning, poverty comes with its own diverse characteristics.
- Incorporate experiences in your teaching which are relevant not only to the lives of middle-class students, but also people who are poor.
- Understand that not everyone learns in the same way, at the same pace, and for the same reason. Differentiate instruction to meet the

needs of all students. Do not assume everyone shares middle-class values and expectations.

- Incorporate life-skills training into your curriculum to help poor students fit into middle-class culture. This can include proper diet, dress, communication skills, and so forth.
- Do not hesitate to reach out to families in poverty by helping them network with others who can provide additional support.

Lessons for Success

Techniques for helping students gain a better understanding of the situations with which they are dealing include using alternative communication paths like metaphors and riddles. This form of indirect teaching promotes thinking and discussion. Caine and Caine (1994) remind us that metaphors are a natural way for the brain to construct new knowledge and acquire meaning. With very young students, child therapists often use puppets as a means of bringing up an unresolved problem. Metaphors can provide hope. When things look negative, students often think, "This is going to go on forever." When encountering a student who has this mind-set, try turning to a metaphor that is based in reality—for example, "Life has its seasons, and it seems like you're in winter right now." Students from poverty will benefit from lessons that teach the "seasons of life," and if they can trust in the cycle of the seasons, they will hopefully learn that, in the long term, things can change.

Sometimes students create their own disabling metaphors. A high school student who was having trouble getting to school on time because of poor sleeping habits once said to me, "I've hit a wall and can't seem to get through it when it comes to getting here on time." I suggested that he change his metaphor by climbing over the wall or drilling a hole through it. I explained that "the wall" could be seen as a stepping-stone to becoming more responsible if he wanted to view it that way. We had a conversation about being able to see life's problems as opportunities to become a better person.

I once wanted to help a student understand the power of her habits. She would come into school and immediately put her head down on the desk. When we talked about why this happened every day, she would say, "Because that's what I always do." One day I gave her a riddle (see box) and we read it together. After every paragraph I asked her, "Who am I?" She would respond, "An enemy?" "A friend?" When I told her "Habits" it was a catalyst for her to consciously analyze her good and bad habits and make choices based on the possible negative and positive outcomes.

Who Am I?

I am your constant companion. I'm your greatest helper or heaviest burden.
I will push you onward or drag you down to failure.
I am completely at your command.
Half the things I do you might just as well turn over to me and
I will be able to do them quickly and correctly.

* * *

I am easily managed—you must merely be firm with me.
Show me exactly how you want something done and
    after a few lessons I will do it automatically.
I am the servant of all great individuals and, alas, of all failures, as well.

* * *

Take me, train me, be firm with me, and I will place the world at your feet.
Be easy with me and I will destroy you.

* * *

Who am I?

—Anonymous

Teaching discipline is done with empathy and precision. To use the analogy of a surgeon, there are no random cuts but rather precise responses which confront the situation and ultimately uplift the student. Having a basic understanding of the potential cause of a behavior can give the teacher the necessary professional objectivity to be effective when teaching discipline. Table 6.1 presents some interventions which may assist in working with students from poverty.

Those who are not aware of how and why they act or feel in a certain way are impoverished. For discipline to be learned, it needs to be taught. Lacking a core awareness of the skills necessary to succeed in different places will create a feeling of alienation and frustration. Helping students who are disadvantaged to use the language of negotiation can become an essential alternative to physical aggression. Giving them choices within limits will assist them in developing internal evaluation of their behaviors. Parents are partners in this process. Communicating the mutual needs of support and respect for each

Table 6.1   Effective Interventions for Students From Poverty

Behavior Related to Poverty	Intervention
Laughs when disciplined. A way to save face in matriarchal poverty.	Tell the student other behaviors that would be more appropriate.
Argues loudly with the teacher. Poverty is participatory, and the culture has a mistrust of authority. Sees the system as inherently unfair.	Don't continue the cycle by arguing with the student. Model respectful talk.
Angry response. Anger is based on fear. The question is what the fear is—loss of face?	Respond in the adult voice. When the student cools down, discuss other phrases that could be used.
Inappropriate or vulgar comments. They rely on casual register, may be unaware of talk or not know formal register.	Put hands over ears, demonstrating disapproval in a nonthreatening manner.
Physically fights. Necessary to survive in poverty. Only knows the language of survival. Does not have language or belief system to use for conflict resolution. Sees himself as less than a man if he does not fight.	Clearly state that fighting will not be tolerated in school. Examine other options the student could live with at school. One option is to not settle the business at school.
Hands always on someone else. Poverty has a heavy reliance on nonverbal data and touch.	Allow them to draw or doodle. Have them hold hands behind their backs while standing in line.
Extremely disorganized. Lack of planning, scheduling, or prioritizing skills not taught in poverty. Also, probably does not have an organized place at home to work or put things.	Teach organization skills. Use a daily assignment book and check with praise and consequences. Have a checklist on wall for each student's organizational needs.
Harms other students. This may be a way of life. Probably a way to get distance. Poverty tends to address issues in the negative.	Explain that this approach is not a choice. Discuss, model, and rehearse acceptable verbal and physical communication skills.
Cheats or steals. Indicative of a weak support system, weak role models, financial need.	Determine cause, and stress that the behavior is disrespectful and illegal, and is not a choice.

SOURCE: Excerpted from "A Framework for Understanding Poverty" (2005), by Ruby K. Payne, Ph.D. Reprinted by permission of Aha! Process, Inc.

other's responsibilities will help bring about a collaborative effort and commitment to each student's progress, as well as a determination to never give up on any student.

UNDERSTANDING CULTURE
AND LINGUISTIC DIFFERENCES

We cannot hope to create safe, cooperative, and inclusive schools without understanding, respecting, and appreciating multiculturalism in our communities. As we are role models for the next generation, it is important first to understand how to overcome cultural differences and then effectively work with these differences in our efforts to reach all students. If our goal is to prepare students to understand and deal with the diverse cultures that comprise our society, then we have the responsibility to understand and address diversity when teaching discipline in our classrooms.

Many children and adults have little understanding of or sensitivity to the impact someone's race, culture, and ethnic background can have on how they deal with problems. We also know that education has not been immune to misunderstanding or even discrimination. Recent studies published by the U.S. Commerce Department show a disturbing trend that both Hispanics and African Americans remain at greater risk of dropping out of school than whites (U.S. Commerce Department Census Bureau, 1997). Asian Americans also face racial challenges. For example, while Asian Americans are much more likely to hold a higher education degree than white Americans, they make on average a lower median salary. Through education, this inequality can be corrected and diversity can remain a strength rather than being synonymous with division. Schools are the natural place to begin bridging these cultural gaps.

Students learn prejudices at an early age and through their life experiences. If they can learn prejudice, they can also unlearn it. Teachers know that differences can sometimes cause conflict within the student and with their peers, and it is important for students to understand that their level of tolerance for others is dependent on their level of flexibility, adaptability, interpersonal skills, and daily experiences. While students and teachers may never be prejudice-free, we can become more understanding and tolerant, if not actually appreciative of, differences among ourselves and our peers while avoiding the cycle of fear and prejudice being passed on to future generations.

Resolving Conflicts Across Cultures: A Case Study

Students tend to feel most comfortable and safe when they are with people similar to themselves. As they form social groups based on their likenesses, they may simultaneously build barriers and exclude other students who are different from them. This exclusion can lead to discipline problems. For example, Eduardo—who is a short, vivacious seventh grader—likes to socialize and play games with his Latino friends during lunch recess at his middle school. They are aggressive in their play, outgoing, and boisterous about their masculinity. I was asked to mediate a problem that arose between Eduardo and a Laotian student, Naang. When I approached Naang, he was refusing to talk, seemed very upset, and was in tears. In his mind, he was being unjustly accused of trying to hit Eduardo. Eduardo was defiant and acted as if everything was "under control." Naang had recently transferred into this middle school, and many other students immediately interpreted his quiet and shy nature as being "stuck up." Some students, including Eduardo, had teased Naang and said hurtful things about his physical features and family members. Naang felt rejected by these students and didn't understand why he was so disliked when he wasn't bothering anyone. In fact, Naang's quiet nature is a desirable quality in his culture, and is taught as a way of showing respect to others.

Before facilitating problem solving between two students from different cultures, it is important that you give some thought to the process. If you try to speed through conflict resolution, you can create an opportunity for new conflicts to arise. To avoid the risk of allowing resentments to further develop, in this case I needed to take the time to allow these students to share their views of the conflict. I also felt it necessary to slow down the conflict resolution process, therefore allowing all of us to develop trust and understanding along the way. My mediation/conflict resolution process consists of the following five steps:

1. Ask students to take turns explaining the way they perceive the situation and how it affected them. If they are too upset to talk, begin by having each one write out his or her point of view. Students from some cultures are reluctant to express emotions until a relationship is established. Direct eye contact can also be difficult and is a sign of disrespect in some cultures.

2. Agree on what the problem actually is and its possible cause(s). Students from some cultures are less comfortable about acknowledging a problem.

3. Brainstorm possible ways to solve the problem. I try to be creative during this process. Students from some cultures are not comfortable building consensus.

4. Agree on what will happen next. Having a written agreement may also be helpful. Students from some cultures feel more comfortable having formal, written documentation.

5. Set a date for follow-up evaluation. I usually attach a clause which rewards progress and gives a logical consequence for regressive behavior. Attitude precedes behavior but students will not change their attitudes just because you tell them to. Personal change takes time and encouragement. In this case, the encouragement came indirectly from me. I offered them a choice and then it was up to them to decide which attitude was preferable.

Our Conversation

Mr. Khalsa: *Eduardo and Naang, I first want to let each of you to tell me in your own words what happened and why you're upset. It's important that you don't interrupt the person talking. You'll both get a chance to give your side of the story. Do you understand?*

Eduardo: *Yeah.*

Naang: (Doesn't speak but, while looking at the ground, nods his head.)

Mr. Khalsa: *Okay, Eduardo, why don't you start.*

Eduardo: *He's crazy. He chased me outside but I stopped quick and he fell. I'm too fast for him. He's always trying to hit me.*

Naang: *That's a lie! He makes fun of me all the time.*

Eduardo: *You're crazy, man.*

Mr. Khalsa: *Wait. First off, Naang, you're breaking the agreement by interrupting Eduardo. I know you're frustrated, but if you can't wait for your turn we'll need to stop our meeting. Eduardo, I want to hear your side of what happened but no name calling. So please continue.*

Eduardo: *There's nothing else to say. I'm not afraid of him. He can't hurt me.*

Naang: *Yes I can.* (Raising his voice with tears in his eyes) *I'm not afraid of you!*

Mr. Khalsa: (Eduardo begins standing up) *Stop. Eduardo, please sit down. I know you're a strong guy and could probably beat up a lot of kids if you wanted to.* (At this point Eduardo sits down while his physical demeanor changes from being aggressive to more relaxed and confident.) *But you know as well as Naang that if you fight in school the consequences are clear. Parents are involved and you're suspended. I want to share something with you. Do you want to hear it?*

Eduardo: *What is it?*

Mr. Khalsa: *Being able to fight takes physical strength, which I know you have. But I also know that to be really strong you need to be able to control your anger with this muscle* (pointing to my head). *Understand? Eduardo, that's when you become a real man. What's up here?*

Eduardo: *My thinking.*

Mr. Khalsa: *Yes. You're right. Now let's hear from Naang.*

Naang: *He makes fun of me and says things about my little brother.*

Mr. Khalsa: *Eduardo, is this true?*

Eduardo: (Thinking for a few seconds) *Yeah.*

Mr. Khalsa: *Great. I really admire someone who tells the truth. What names do you call Naang?*

Eduardo: *Stupid. Crazy. Stuff like that.*

Mr. Khalsa: *Naang, is this true?*

Naang: *Yes. And he calls my brother Chinese food.*

Mr. Khalsa: *Why do you call Naang and his brother these names?*

Eduardo: *Because he tries to hit me.*

Mr. Khalsa: *Naang, is this true?*

Naang: *Yes. But I do that because he won't stop making fun of me.*

Mr. Khalsa: *Okay. I think we're getting somewhere because you're both brave enough to tell the truth. Now I'd like both of you to try something. Eduardo, I'd like you to start by giving Naang some advice.*

Eduardo: *What kind of advice?*

Mr. Khalsa: *Good question. I want you to tell Naang what he should do if you're in a bad mood or not feeling strong up here* (pointing to my head) *and call him a name.*

Eduardo: *Just ignore me and walk away. Don't run after me and try to hit me.*

Mr. Khalsa: *Did you hear that, Naang?*

Naang: *Yes.*

Mr. Khalsa:	*Good. Now I'd like you to give Eduardo some advice that may help him control his thinking and therefore stop making fun of you.*
Naang:	(After a few minutes of not saying anything) *You should think about how it feels to have someone make fun of you.*
Mr. Khalsa:	*That sounds like good advice. What do you think, Eduardo?*
Eduardo:	(As he slumps back into his chair) *Well, that would be good if I cared how people feel but I really don't. I'm not a feely type of guy.*
Mr. Khalsa:	*Okay. Let's forget about feely for a minute. Does anyone ever make fun of you at school or maybe at home?*
Eduardo:	*No.*
Mr. Khalsa:	*Never? You've never had anyone make fun of you?*
Eduardo:	*My uncle calls me names like "shrimp" and "skin flea" but he can't hurt me. I just call him a "fathead" and run.*
Mr. Khalsa:	*You want him to call you names?*
Eduardo:	*No. But he does it anyway.*
Mr. Khalsa:	*Well, Naang gave you some good advice and you gave him good advice as well. This is what I'd like to propose. For the next week, stay away from each other. You know how to do that. And think about the advice each one of you gave each other for solving this conflict. I want to meet with both of you next Friday at noon to see how the week went. If you stay away from each other, I'm going to tell you something you'll both like. But if you get into a conflict again, then the vice principal will have to take over. Agreed?*
Naang:	*Okay.*
Eduardo:	*Yeah.*

The following Friday, when I was at their school, Naang saw me in the hallway in the morning and approached me with a smile on his face. He asked if we were going to meet at noon. I told him I would pull him out of class to meet and thanked him for remembering. I also saw Eduardo, who said he wanted to tell me how the week went. I asked him to wait until noon. When we met, I invited the vice principal to join us. Both boys said they had stayed away from each other and that they were both feeling better about the situation. The vice principal expressed her satisfaction and desire to see this continue.

I then told them that for their efforts I had a dollar bill to give them that could be spent on a dessert at lunchtime. The problem needing to be solved was how to give each of them fifty cents. Eduardo quickly said he could make change and give Naang fifty cents. Naang thought that was a good idea because Eduardo's table got lunch first. I gave Eduardo the dollar bill and told them we'll meet again the following Friday to see how their week went. They both smiled, thanked me for the money, and walked to lunch together.

Over time, I saw an attitude and behavioral change. In this case, brainstorming possible options for solving the problem involved asking each student to give the other advice. Sometimes I like putting the student in a teacher's role. This strategy often helps them to become more rational. Unless a student is rational, it is useless trying to problem solve. Note the encouragement I gave was offering "something good." I occasionally will give a dollar as a reward because I understand money is a very strong positive reinforcer for students (as well as adults). I also manipulated the situation so that they would need to work together to receive the money and therefore share in a positive life experience. My purpose in doing this was to enhance their connected self-esteem and change a cycle of negative reinforcing behaviors and attitudes. The following week we shot some baskets together in the gym.

When using this model of conflict resolution, being sensitive to each student's cultural, racial, or ethnic differences also entails keeping in mind the similarities which are equally as strong. All students want to be successful in school and gain competencies and skills. They want to have fun, make friends, be accepted, and feel part of the "school community." These powerful needs are clamoring to be expressed and actualized. The teacher is the key to opening up new doors for this to occur in all students.

Breaking Bread

There are some traditions that connect all cultures. An experienced middle school adjustment counselor and colleague calls this connecting strategy "breaking bread." It is not unusual to see Tim Murphy sitting with one or two students who have recently been in a conflict or are gearing up for one, sharing an orange or crackers with them. He understands that before any problem solving can occur a relationship needs to be established. Regardless of students' race or ethnic background, Mr. Murphy also understands that all middle school–aged children can be moody, sensitive, oppositional, rude, impulsive, and self-absorbed. They all share these traits, along with a vast appetite for food and physical activity. Sharing food with a student sends the overt message, "I care enough about you that I will feed you." It also sends the covert message of connection and family. All cultures hear these messages and respond in a positive way.

Relationship Building

As discussed in Chapter 1, building relationships with your students creates a foundation upon which all other disciplinary procedures can be built. Many students who have difficulty following classroom rules and procedures seem to feel that their teachers don't like or understand them. One study (Garibaldi, 1992) found that 60 percent of African American males believed that their teachers had failed to push them to succeed. Fostering caring relationships with all students is imperative, but this is especially so with the students who are receiving the majority of detentions and reports of misbehavior. African Americans tend to be people oriented and take great care in establishing and maintaining relationships (Franklin, 1992). African American students need to feel that their teachers have an interest in their lives both in and outside of the school setting. One way this can be achieved is by creating time to have informal talks with your students. Educating yourself about the contemporary cultural norms of the African American students' major interest areas (e.g., music and sports) will help bridge the gap between teacher and student. For example, a few years ago one of my students told me that they saw a "Sikh" man who looked a lot like me in a music video. I asked whether they could record it the next time it was shown on TV and bring it to class. A few days later one of the students brought the video in. The artist's name was "Ludacris" and the song was "Going to Atlanta." There was a Sikh man in the video who had a small but prominent role (our physical similarities stopped at the beard and turban). I watched the video with the class and for the remainder of the year joked with the students about how it was really me in the video. This opportunity for building relationships with my African American and Hispanic students served me well for the rest of the year.

Managing the Classroom

Davis and Jordan (1994) found that a higher percentage of suspensions occurred when the teacher was engaged in discipline-related matters versus academic discourse. In suburban school classrooms, the majority of teacher statements focus on academics. Conversely, in urban classrooms, the teacher's comments revolve around managing the behavior of students, therefore resulting in fewer opportunities for academic engagement. To be certain that culturally and linguistically diverse students receive a high percentage of accountable talk or instruction that challenges them to use their higher level thinking skills, teachers can observe the rate at which they call on students, ask open-ended questions, and focus on academics. Incorporating auditory, visual, and kinesthetic tasks which encourage student movement will also promote the successful and active learning of all students. Observations can be achieved by asking a colleague to watch you teach while taking notes on the content and frequency of your interactions.

Feeling Connected

As children grow into adolescence, they will experience many dramatic shifts in their connections to family, friends, and the world around them. This stage is often disruptive for both parents and teenagers. During adolescence, the matrix of connectedness will switch from home to school. All teenagers need to feel adequate satisfaction from connections in their school lives. Students who have been less successful in school are also less likely to join or be affiliated with school clubs, organizations, and athletic teams. Problems that can arise from this feeling of disconnectedness from the whole school community include some of the following behaviors:

- Does not communicate easily and is unable to listen to others and understand their point of view
- Actively avoids social situations and is unaware of others' interests or needs
- Seldom, if ever, volunteers to help others
- Acts uncomfortable around teachers, or else constantly seeks their attention

Students of color can become cynical about the purpose of community activities if they are not an integral part of the process. Teachers can be instrumental in helping diverse students to feel a sense of belonging in their school environments. When building relationships, interests and talents will become known. Actively motivate students to use their artistic, musical, athletic, leadership, and other talents for the entertainment and improvement of the whole community. Students who are sensitive to social issues can be encouraged to participate in a class or school social change project. Students who have a talent for dancing, singing, or movement can create a "school cheer." Helping to lessen students' opposition and defiance toward school activities will increase their ability to participate and ensure they feel more connected to their school community.

Personal Connections

I once asked my students whether they watched the World Series. I then explained, "When you are watching a game you are a spectator. You are not on the baseball field running, throwing, and catching the ball. But in the classroom you need to fully participate or be in the game in order to learn. Learning is not a spectator sport. Learning requires active participation." There are techniques teachers use to assist students in the process of active involvement.

Before introducing a lesson, skillful teachers understand the importance of providing a hook or connection that will make the lesson personal. Teachers want to find some experience or background knowledge to which students can connect the new information. Elementary teachers may show pictures or share a personal experience prior to reading a story in order to pique the students' interest and involvement in the learning process. Knowing your students' backgrounds and interests is an essential component of this strategy. Townsend (2000) says it is imperative that educators develop creative and genuine techniques for gaining insight into the lives of Hispanic, African American, and ethnically diverse students. This insight can enhance the traditional curriculum, making it more meaningful to those students. She suggests interests can be connected to various aspects of the popular market, such as the increasingly sophisticated video games available. Mark Delude, a former middle school science teacher, incorporated the use of computer-assisted instruction and PowerPoint presentations to teach research and presentation skills. Roger, an African American student who had a severe reading disability and was caught in a cycle of sleeping in the class, was also highly adept at video game technology. He became highly engaged in Mr. Delude's science classes, incorporating music, moving figures, and animated text into his PowerPoint presentations.

> We understand that when a student is engaged in learning, they have little interest in or time for misbehavior.

The Cultural Divide

Franklin (1992) points out that cultural conflicts are potentially problematic when it comes to diverse students' participation and engagement in public schools. One common cultural norm for many students is being comfortable with multitasking in their home and community. For example, they may be involved in many conversations while eating, studying, watching television, listening to music, and so on. This natural interpersonal strength can cause problems in a traditional classroom setting where the students are asked to work at the same pace, and in the same way. Some students can be seen as disruptive or uncooperative for attempting to engage in multiple activities or learning styles. Classrooms that incorporate differentiated instruction strategies support the interpersonal behaviors students have mastered and need to express in school.

Some culturally and ethnically diverse students have a natural tendency to interact with speakers during a lecture or "sermon." This tradition is also referred to as "call and response." Most of our traditional classrooms expect students to sit passively, looking at the teacher without speaking or commenting. Some students may be labeled as rude or seen as purposefully distracting the teacher or "talking back" when they engage in this call-and-response behavior. I have discovered that this behavior can potentially be invigorating and motivating. If used correctly, it can facilitate students' engagement in the learning process. I have used the call-and-response mode of communication to create both a motivating and enjoyable learning climate in class. When teaching vocabulary words in a science class, I write them on a transparency which is projected on to a screen using an overhead projector. I then begin the activity by striking a beat on a small hand-held drum. Students are then instructed to repeat the word and the meaning after me, in rhythm with the beat. As students become comfortable with the activity, drumbeats and volume can become more complicated and engaging.

Role Models

In the Springfield schools, where the student population is predominantly African American and Hispanic, I have observed Caucasian middle and high school students trying to "act Black," which is perceived as being "cool" and acceptable. Conversely, African American students may purposely resist certain behaviors in class that are perceived as "acting White," such as speaking standard English or asking questions. This defiance toward certain school rules and expectations may result from a cultural disconnect between the African American students and the dominant school culture.

Although speaking nonstandard English can be seen by teachers as defiant and rude, understanding the power and comfort African American youth feel when speaking in their regional dialect can avoid unnecessary power struggles between teachers and students. For example, terms such as "homey" and "dawg" connote friendship and closeness, but can also be misinterpreted as being disrespectful. Another potential communication problem area is the loud volume and tone in which many African American students speak. In a classroom where students are expected to use quieter tones or their "library voices," loud tones can become annoying and are perceived as a violation of the classroom rules and expectations. Helping students understand how to adapt their language to fit different settings, or "code-switching," can support successful behavior in the mainstream community (Perry, 1993).

ADHD: A MISTAKEN DISORDER

False Assumptions

Assumptions are unexamined beliefs. Educators who consider themselves professionals recognize that each of us brings with us a set of beliefs about the students we teach and the teachers with whom we work. Some of our beliefs are helpful and others are harmful. As professional educators, it is important to become aware of our unexamined beliefs by objectively determining whether they are based in fact, bias, or stereotyping. For example, a child (like many young, healthy boys) can be overactive without being hyperactive. Assumptions can have a powerful influence on our relationship with our students. Our ability to reach out and teach all students is directly impacted by our sensitivity and understanding of their academic, emotional, and behavioral needs.

Attention deficit hyperactivity disorder (ADHD) is believed by most experts in the field to be a neurobiological disorder. It is characterized by degrees of impulsivity, inattention, and hyperactivity. Environmental factors can also influence the severity of the disorder. A student who has been diagnosed with ADHD often has difficulty in academics, social interactions, and self-control. Dr. Russell Barkely, one of the leading experts in the field of neurology, characterizes ADHD as involving problems with disinhibition (ability to control emotions and ability to wait) and with sustaining attention, effort, and persistence. In the United States, ADHD affects approximately 5 percent of the population, or around ten million people.

Unfortunately, I occasionally will hear people referring to students with ADHD as children who were just brought up with "a lack of discipline." A colleague once told me that "these kids just need to be quickly punished like any other kid who misbehaves." My colleague's inaccurate assumption will then become an expectation based on a false understanding of this disorder. It is imperative that we know and understand our students and their disabilities before reaching any conclusions. Remaining open to new information can only increase our effectiveness. Our open-mindedness will give us a more accurate picture of how we can effectively teach discipline.

If we are to follow a professional standard that enables us to become professional educators, fact rather than emotion must act as our guide. In fact, as I previously mentioned, the term "discipline" comes from the same Latin root word as "disciple," or "someone who follows your example and teaching." Let's think about this relationship when we make decisions on how best to correct student behavior. Are we modeling thinking and acting behaviors we want students to emulate? Or are students likely to see our behavior as an example of what we often criticize in their behavior, such as impulsivity and reacting from emotional frustration?

Parents as Partners

Teachers who have students diagnosed with ADHD in their classrooms have a challenging responsibility. Knowing what not to do is as important as knowing what to do. Teachers cannot and should not diagnose ADHD or tell parents their child has ADHD and should see a doctor. ADHD is a medical diagnosis. The role of a teacher is to share objective observations and concerns about their students with parents. Parents should understand that it is not unusual for children to have several overlapping diagnoses such as ADHD and learning disabilities (LDs) or depression. When it comes to performance, this condition can be very frustrating for teachers and parents because one day students with ADHD are capable of doing the work, and the next they are not. But we do know that a behaviorist program is more effective in dealing with behaviors associated with ADHD than a psychotherapeutic program.

Because ADHD is seen by many as a biological disorder caused by a chemical imbalance in the area of the brain responsible for attention and activity, often a medical intervention is effective in increasing the ability to attend and inhibit or control behaviors. Cylert and Ritalin are the most commonly prescribed medications for ADHD. The use of medication for students with ADHD is a controversial topic. Some parents are reluctant to use medication to help deal with their child's behavior. Concern over the possible side effects of medication, such as insomnia and irritability, can be a factor. Parents should be informed about the interventions, and information is available to them so they can make informed and sometimes difficult decisions.

A very insightful book on attention deficit disorder is *Driven to Distraction*, written by Dr. Ned Hallowell and Dr. John Ratey (1994), who both have ADHD themselves. They point out that people with ADHD don't so much have a difficult time focusing, but rather focus on too many things at once. As a pair of eyeglasses corrects one's vision and brings a picture into focus, certain medication used in the treatment of ADHD can help keep a student more focused in school.

The majority of children who are diagnosed with ADHD grow up to be adults with this disorder, although the behaviors may change or manifest themselves differently as the student moves into adolescence and adulthood. Common symptoms of students with ADHD include poor self-image, lack of inner control, impulsivity, erratic academic performance, poor social skills, forgetfulness, poor organizational skills, underachievement, attraction to high stimulation and high-risk behaviors, moodiness, distractibility, and difficulty in following through.

Children with ADHD have ability and skill, and know what to do in class, but have difficulty demonstrating or acting on it with consistency. I believe if we are going to be effective in helping students with ADHD succeed in the classroom, as well as feel part of the school community, we must remember to focus our attention of the positive aspects and traits associated with ADHD. You might think this is a contradiction in terms, but this is not so. Some of these traits and behaviors include the following:

- High energy
- Spontaneity
- Resourcefulness
- Caring
- Risk taking
- Empathy
- Inquisitiveness
- Imaginativeness
- Creativity

Seven Principles in Managing Behavior Associated With ADHD

1. More Immediate Feedback and Consequences

Students with ADHD require more feedback about their acceptable behaviors. Feedback must also be clear and specific—for example, "Thank you for standing in line without touching someone." Physical affection and tangible rewards such as extra privileges can help change cycles. Behavior management that systematically reinforces positive behavior

---

(Continued)

Seven Principles (Continued)

can be introduced. Regardless of the feedback, more immediate and more frequent intervention is more effective.

2. More Salient Consequences

There is a need for an increase in clear consequences to motivate students to engage in work and follow classroom rules and expectations. Social praise is often not sufficient, but a reliance on extrinsic consequences needs to be reduced by introducing intrinsic reinforcers such as pleasure of reading, pleasing others, and following rules. Initially these rewards will not likely to govern behavior, however; the nature of the disorder dictates that larger and more significant consequences may be necessary to support inner control (e.g., a note home, a self-monitoring checklist).

3. Positives Before Negatives

You should act, not talk when dealing with the behavior of children with ADHD in the classroom. When situations arise, respond with a measure of professional objectivity. Catch the student doing the right thing and avoid the criticism trap.

4. Act With Consistency

Be consistent with your responses each day the behavior occurs, as responding consistently across different settings and places is important. Don't give up too soon if you don't see a change in the negative behavior. When working with other teachers, spend time discussing the need for consistency among all team members.

5. Anticipate Problems

Ask when the defiant, disruptive behavior occurs. Is it during recess, lunch, or transition times? What happens before the behavior is noticed? Put your observations to good use and then come up with a plan that is shared with the student. For example: (a) Stop before transition time. (b) Review rules and ask student to repeat rules. (c) Review positive consequences when rules are followed and negative ones when they are not. Proactive observation can reduce problem behavior and give the student the message that you are on top of the situation.

6. Keeping a Perspective

Be careful to not lose your self-control when working with a student with ADHD. These students need prompting, incentives, and refocusing to stay on task. In order to intervene effectively, it is imperative to maintain some psychological distance from the student's behavior. Remember, ADHD is a psychological disorder, not a behavior.

It is important to note that not all students with ADHD have the characteristics of hyperactivity. There is a category of students who have the predominately inattentive type of ADHD. Many of these children have difficulty sustaining attention, may seem to daydream a lot, and have accompanying learning disabilities.

7. Start Each Day Anew

Let go of any built-up frustration and resentment you may be holding on to from the previous day's challenges. To be an effective teacher of discipline, you must learn from your mistakes and repeat your successes. Maintaining a positive mental attitude is the basis for your effectiveness.

Positive Interventions

Effective practices when working with students with ADHD include many accommodations that are also effective when working with students with LDs in an inclusive classroom setting. Behavior problems associated with ADHD often cannot totally be resolved but they can be minimized. The following list includes some of the accommodations students with ADHD and/or LDs need to succeed.

- Assistance through transitions
- Learning style accommodations
- Extra physical and psychological space
- A low-distractibility work area
- Choices
- Predictable routines and schedules
- Consistency among team members
- Differentiated instructional strategies
- Assistance with coping skills
- A social skills curriculum
- Possible medical interventions
- Opportunities to exercise and release energy
- Systematic muscle relaxation training
- Wholesome diet (no refined sugar)
- Teacher-guided instruction
- Cooperative learning strategies
- Cueing, prompting, and reminding
- Assistance with organization

- Behavior contracts
- Positive reinforcement

NOTE: *The Inclusive Classroom: A Practical Guide for Educators* (Khalsa, 2005) provides in-depth strategies/interventions and guidance on helping students with LDs.

Summary Reports

When working with a team of teachers, specialists, and parents, writing a summary report on a student's progress and decisions agreed upon will help keep everyone aware of the intervention plan that is being implemented. Typically, the special educator or school counselor will write the summary, with copies given to parents, team members, and any other professionals outside of school who are involved in caring for the student. The following example of a summary report was written for a seventh-grade student who has been diagnosed with ADHD and LD.

Robert has been a student at John F. Kennedy Middle School for the past two years. He is a capable boy, with strengths in physical education and math. Robert has identified learning disabilities and ADHD, and a history of impulsive and highly distractible behavior. It is a challenge for him to focus his attention even in small-group settings. He has a constant need to talk and make distracting noises, which has been problematic in that he interrupts the teacher and his classmates. He has difficulty waiting to tell or talk about things that come to mind regardless of whether they are on or off topic. Consequently, his teachers and classmates become very impatient and exasperated with his interruptions, and it has been my observation that he has developed a self-concept as the "class trouble-maker." Class work has been inconsistent over the two years due to the above behaviors.

Robert's parents were at first reluctant to try a suggested prescribed medication due to their feeling that Robert "would grow out of it." On occasion, Robert's father would come to school and lecture him on how to act in class. Immediately after his father left the school, Robert would demonstrate increased self-control, but this lasted for only a short period of time before he returned to his usual behaviors.

Last month, Robert's parents decided to give him his medication in the morning before school. Since Robert has been taking a dose of medication before he comes to school, we have observed a significant improvement during the morning classes (8:05–12:05). There has been less impulsive behavior, and he is much better able to inhibit his blurting out noises and inappropriate comments. He is also less defensive when given feedback about his behavior. Due to his ADHD and learning disability in short-term memory, he still has a need to ask a lot of questions and becomes easily confused.

Robert's afternoon teachers have suggested considering a second dose of medication in the afternoon at school to see if there would be any improvement in behavior during the afternoon classes. His afternoons continue to be inconsistent. Some days he has a lot of difficulty controlling impulsive behavior and staying on task, other days he does better. His afternoon teachers' main concerns are Robert's difficulty listening, following directions, completing assignments, and becoming overly defiant when given feedback on his behavior. Robert's parents are discussing the additional dose with their family physician.

As we discussed at our last meeting, the following interventions are currently being used or will be provided for Robert's success in school:

- Preferential seating (in front seat close to the teacher)
- Robert's assignment book to be checked daily and initialed last period by the classroom paraprofessional and parent when Robert comes home
- One-on-one verbal and nonverbal cueing, redirecting, and signaling to stay on task
- Self-monitoring checklist to be used for the afternoon classes
- Frequent opportunities to work with a learning buddy
- Opportunities to have extra time on the computer as a reward for completed class work
- Robert knows that when he feels overwhelmed, he can ask to speak with his special education teacher or adjustment counselor
- Continued special education services through pull-out as needed in reading and math
- Effectiveness of interventions to be evaluated at the end of the month

ENHANCING THE POTENTIAL OF ALL STUDENTS

As teachers gain insight into the cultural norms and internal behavioral needs of their students, and apply meaningful and effective management strategies, we can increase the learning potential of students who often feel disconnected from their daily school experience. By strengthening relationships and taking advantage of family and community resources, we can help to build a foundation for success with individuals who may previously have had negative experiences with school personnel. Increasing proactive decision making while teaching in a diverse classroom will enhance the inclusion and success of all students.

Leadership and Helping Others

I recently attended a luncheon at Fitchburg State College for teachers in training. The keynote speaker, 2003 Massachusetts Teacher of the Year Jeff Ryan, was asked to share some wisdom for the student teachers to take away with them. He said, "I could tell you reading, math, history, and the sciences are all very important subjects to teach our children. I could also tell you the arts are essential, but I believe the most important lesson we could teach our students is that they are not the center of the universe." He proceeded to explain how our future leaders must understand the importance of helping others in need and develop the capacity to see beyond their small worlds. I have found this to be true as well. A teenager who can gain satisfaction from connections in his life that bring him "out of himself" will not need to be the center of attention but instead will develop a desire to attend to others. Leaders express concern for others as well as taking care of their own needs.

Teachers can create opportunities for all students—regardless of their abilities or disabilities—to work and play together for the greater good. When I taught a class of adolescent students with emotional and mental disabilities, the tendency was for them to obsess on their issues (and they had many). During one holiday season, I decided to create a Helping the Homeless project. It entailed collecting food and blankets for the local survival center. I witnessed a positive change in the behaviors of some of the most depressed and aggressive students after they participated in this project.

Jeff Ryan showed us slides of a group of his high school students who he had recently taken to Peru. Most of the pictures were of a poor school community of children standing on dirt floor classrooms with shining smiles on their faces. These types of experience can change lives. Offering lessons of cooperation where individuals seek outcomes beneficial to themselves and others will build a sense of connectedness and self-esteem which many of our students lack. Our students must see to it that they are in the right place with the right people who can help them recognize and release their potential in a manner that enhances human life itself.

Building a community of learners begins with identifying the potential issues that can undermine trust and security among all students. Directly addressing the issue of bullying is the most effective approach in dealing with this negative dynamic. Teachers must examine and state their position on issues that are relevant to developing a policy against bullying. I believe that, if teachers and parents are given this forum to discuss and openly say what they think, there will be an opportunity to genuinely engage in the discussion of what needs to be done. When this can occur, the chances then become much higher for a committed, wholehearted approach to stop bullying. This "whole community approach" should include discussing strategies with students such as those I've included, which can empower the potential victim and send the message to the aggressor that bullying behavior will never be tolerated in your school.

Creating safe and caring classrooms is an essential goal which enables all students to feel comfortable expressing their feelings and concerns. All students must know that they can make mistakes without being ridiculed, deal with their differences constructively, and disagree respectfully. Supporting these standards is also making a commitment to support social responsibility. We want to encourage our students to direct their energies in a positive and constructive manner while acting on their concerns in ways that make a positive difference for themselves and others. We want our students to develop the convictions and skills to shape a more just and peaceful school community and world.

Managing Your Stress: Help for Educators

AVOIDING BURNOUT

It's 7:45 a.m. Ms. Montrose worked late last night preparing activities for the next unit on China. She checks her mailbox and reads a note asking her to make sure the attendance sheets are filled out properly. There is a reminder notice about an important staff meeting after school and a note from the principal: "Please see me at your earliest convenience." She goes to make copies of photos for her students. The copier is down so she'll have to improvise. Ms. Montrose heads off to her classroom before the students get off the bus.

Ms. Montrose looks at the clock and sees that she has about ten minutes to write the day's agenda on the board, turn on the computers, check her e-mail, and organize the material needed for the first activity. She's still upset about an incident that occurred at the end of the day with one of her "problem students." She told him they would need to talk about it before the start of class. She gets a call from the office. The parent of the "problem student" has unexpectedly come to school and is waiting in the office to speak with her. She wonders if this is why the principal wants to speak with her. So much is on her mind and the students haven't even arrived yet.

Tonight she'll need to go to the copy shop after the evening class she's taking for her master's degree. The cost of copying the activities will be more than she can afford, but what other choice does she have? It is January and she is really looking forward to the weekend. She knew teaching was going to be a challenge but didn't expect it to be so tiring.

We know that the profession of teaching is a challenging one and that it is one of the most stressful occupations in America. Our profession is unique in that we can plan the best lesson and have everything organized yet, with little or no notice, must make changes. Why? Because we are dealing with human behavior, which is subject to change at any time. Something happens on the bus, in the hallway, at home, or during the class that causes a total change in plans. We also know that the new members of our profession are most vulnerable to the negative effects of career stress.

Burnout can affect all teachers, regardless of experience and grade level. Burnout is not a sudden event but occurs over a period of time due to an accumulation of stresses that, in time, can turn even the most dedicated teacher of discipline into a disheartened cynic. I've noticed over the many years of being in this noble profession that it is often the idealistic and best-intentioned teachers of discipline who are most affected.

Signs of Burnout

Becoming aware of the warning signals or signs of burnout is the first step toward avoiding this state of physical, mental, and emotional exhaustion. The following are the most common symptoms.

- Irritability
- Illness
- Defensiveness
- Impatience
- Alcohol and drug abuse
- Overeating
- Loss of appetite
- Sleep disturbances
- Anxiety
- Sexual dysfunction
- Absenteeism
- Negative mental attitude
- Low self-esteem
- Lack of energy

If any of these symptoms are consistently part of your life, please spend some time with this chapter because, although any teacher can experience burnout, it is not inevitable. The stress that is at the root of burnout begins slowly due to inadequate coping skills and a lack of supportive environments. It is up to you to protect yourself from burnout because it will not occur without notice and will not leave overnight.

I offer suggestions and strategies teachers are using that can be helpful in learning how to successfully cope with the demands of your profession. You will learn how to identify the warning signals your body and mind set off, which can help you avoid the harmful effects of burnout. You will understand the importance of building a supportive workplace and how to avoid the unavoidable by taking control of your well-being.

New Teachers and Burnout

Novice teachers are more vulnerable to burnout for a variety of reasons. Some of these reasons can be avoided while others cannot.

- They lack administrative support for a difficult new profession.
- They are often asked to teach the most difficult students.
- They lack necessary curriculum materials.
- They lack the experience necessary for effective decision making.
- They are asked to deal with the same demands as experienced teachers.
- They can experience a loss of enthusiasm for the teaching profession when faced with the reality of the classroom.

How you manage your professional life will determine the degree to which you will be an effective educator. Let's first determine what you know and do not know about stress management (see Lesson Box 7.1).

How Did You Do?

1. Writing in a daily journal can be an excellent method of releasing stress from your day's work. Feelings are a product of our thoughts, and writing down the day's events is a strategy for letting go of stress-producing thoughts.

2. Drinking alcohol is a temporary cure for a long-term problem. Alcohol is a depressant and won't help you solve your problems.

3. Being informed about the world's news is important. But beginning and ending your day by watching the news, which focuses on daily disasters and political problems, can only heighten a sense of despair.

4. Asking for advice from a trusted colleague or friend can help neutralize tension built up over a period of time. Being able to get

Lesson Box 7.1   Common Stress Management Options

Below is a list of common stress management options people may use following a difficult day at school. Check "True" or "False" based on your understanding of the effectiveness of each possible stress management strategy.

	True	*False*
1. Writing in a daily journal will relieve stress.		
2. Drinking alcohol will relieve stress.		
3. Watching the news will relieve stress.		
4. Asking for advice will relieve stress.		
5. Smoking will relieve stress.		
6. Meditating or praying will relieve stress.		
7. Getting up two hours earlier will relieve stress.		
8. Indulging in a sweet treat will relieve stress.		
9. Working harder will relieve stress.		
10. Watching television will relieve stress.		

advice can also provide an alternative viewpoint on how to solve previously unsolvable problems.

5. Smoking constricts oxygen to the brain and can create a temporary feeling of relaxation. But, as we all now know, smoking is a very serious health concern and certainly not a solution to stress or any of life's problems.

6. Any activity, such as meditation and prayer, that can help you control your thoughts and create a sound perspective on your workday difficulties is very healthy.

7. If you get up early to partake in a meaningful and positive experience such as exercising, reading inspirational material, or sipping tea while listening to beautiful music, then this strategy may be helpful. But sleep deprivation for the purpose of completing work will only compound stress.

8. Overindulging in sweets can be harmful to your body and mind. Eating sweets may give you a temporary boost of energy but in a short time you may feel even more fatigued.

9. Working more efficiently and smarter rather than harder will relieve stress.

10. Watching television can provide a temporary escape, but beware of the couch potato syndrome, which has never solved any of life's problems.

Stress Awareness

We live with a certain amount of stress in our daily lives and, as long as it does not get to the "toxic" level, stress can help keep us focused and motivated. Stress becomes problematic when it takes over a person's life. Dealing with problematic behaviors can be stressful and lead to exhaustion. What happens when we start to become "stressed out"? Let's use the analogy of a frayed electric cord. The fabrics wrapped around copper wires become exposed from overuse and eventually either start a fire or blow a fuse. Similarly, our nerves—which are a network of 72,000 "wires" connecting and carrying messages back and forth to the brain—can become weak or "frayed" and then blow a fuse or burn out.

One of the causes of frayed nerves is the constant secretion of adrenaline, which is triggered by feelings such as anger, fear, and loss of control. This creates a false sense of power which in turn leads to toxic stress, causing the body to run on empty energy. Before we look at steps toward stress release and maintaining a strong nervous system, let's determine your susceptibility to distress and burnout (see Lesson Box 7.2).

Lesson Box 7.2   Self-Evaluation

Read each statement and determine how it applies to your life as a teacher by checking "Yes" or "No." Decide on how many work days a week you think each statement could apply to you.

	Yes	No
1. I feel I have the energy to do my work as an effective teacher.		
2. I use effective discipline strategies that educate my students and support their self-esteem.		
3. I look forward to seeing all my students and enjoy being with them.		
4. I use efficient time management strategies to take care of my non-instructional responsibilities (e.g., grading papers, reports, phone calls).		
5. I maintain a positive mental attitude with my colleagues.		
6. I effectively communicate my needs and concerns to my colleagues and administration staff.		
7. I feel friendly support from my colleagues and administrators.		
8. I have other hobbies or interests for which I make time after work.		
9. My students are motivated and participate in the learning process.		
10. My classes are filled with interesting and engaging lessons.		

How Did You Do?

This informal self-evaluation can give you a sense of how you're managing your stress. If you decide that being a teacher of discipline is your calling, then it is imperative that you have an understanding of how to manage your energy by staying in the "healthy zone" for preventative burnout. If most of these statements ring true, it means you're managing your stress well. If a few statements are not occurring during the working week, there may be problems at school that you can manage more effectively. But your overall stress management skills are still pretty good. If you find yourself saying "no" to about half of the statements, you need to take time to deal with some of these issues before they become overwhelming in your professional life.

Answering "yes" to less than half of these statements indicates that you are in danger of burnout. But don't be discouraged. As I said, burnout can be avoided if you commit yourself to changing some negative habits by replacing them with positive ones. First, decide which areas of work you want to begin changing. Then talk with an experienced teacher and seek support for your new commitment. Follow the advice I offer in the rest of this chapter and manage your stress, and you will consequently feel healthier and become more effective in changing the lives of your students.

Work Stressors You Can't Control

We understand that, in the teaching profession—as in all professions—there will always be issues and problems that are unavoidable and uncontrollable. One of the most important and frustrating lessons learned in your professional life is being able to recognize the stressful situations that you can change and those that you can't. Accepting the existence of situations that can't be controlled, at least during the current school year, is a practical approach and solution. Understanding what you can and cannot control is a critical step in avoiding burnout. This acceptance does not mean that those issues don't really exist or are not important. It also doesn't mean that you will not deal with the problem at some time in the future. What it does mean is that you are choosing a healthy approach to your current teaching responsibilities.

For example, a situation where a student comes to school upset because of problems occurring at home cannot be controlled.

> Focus on what is really important: being the best teacher possible in spite of the problems you can't solve.

Realizing that you are not alone, in that other teachers face this same problem but have learned to adjust, can be comforting. Accepting what you can't control and learning what you can change will make your school life much easier and more rewarding.

Facing a career with many troubling demands is difficult. But challenges such as not being able to make the changes you feel are necessary exist in other careers as well. Before you allow yourself to burn out, consider practicing the preventive stress-releasing strategies many educators are using to maintain their effectiveness in the classroom (see the section starting on page 168).

Stressors You Can Control

The problems listed in Activity Sheet 7.1 can arise in a typical school year and can effectively be controlled with some effort and creative thinking. Each problem may be one you are struggling with now or may be a problem you'll face in the future. Being an effective teacher of discipline involves being imaginative and able to be proactive. One attribute all teachers possess is the ability to problem solve. Dealing with problems that can be solved will reduce stress and increase the positive impact you have on your students. For each problem discussed, I've included a few practical solutions, as well as a space for your creative problem solving.

Protecting Your Energy

You need energy for working, playing, staying focused, and relaxing. One way you can view the cause of stress in your school life is by understanding how the people you interact with—both students and adults—can be neutral, give you energy, or attempt to steal your energy. The people who are neutral usually are occupied with something and their attention is elsewhere. Those who give you energy are actively involved in making a successful experience out of the activity in which you are mutually engaged. It could be as simple as giving a smile, saying hello while passing in the hallway, or asking relevant questions and participating in a class.

The "energy snatchers" often don't know how to regenerate their own energy and therefore attempt to draw energy from others. For example, a student who is feeling ignored or bored may try to steal energy by making an inappropriate comment or behaving in a way that gets attention. An adult who is low on energy may start complaining, with no desire to find a solution.

An Alternative

Actually, no one can steal energy from you unless you let them. Most successful teachers of discipline have to learn ways to protect their energy or they quickly become victims of burnout. Contrary to feeling burned out, there is a feeling of balance, of inner strength, that we feel when we are centered. Schools place a great value on the development of cognitive, rational, and intellectual processes. In order to actively and successfully engage in the activities that promote these aspects of education, we also need to feel in control of our emotions, behaviors, and thoughts—or feel centered. Energy snatchers can pull you off center. The goal in school is not to always remain centered, but rather to return to your center in a reasonable amount of time after being pulled off by an event or situation.

The following questions will help you gain an awareness of the ways people tend to have their energy depleted. You may want to write down your responses to help you reflect on your answers.

1. Ask yourself, "What thoughts, feelings and sensations in my body am I aware of when a student is verbally attacking me, or a colleague aggressively questions a decision I have made?" Common answers may include "a feeling in the pit of my stomach," "my head begins to hurt," "I become defensive," or "I get angry."

2. What are the most common ways in which you let others steal energy from you—for example, trying to defend your decision, needing to be right, feeling personally put down by what others say, putting others down?

3. What are some of the early warning signals which help you identify energy snatchers—for example, whining, critical or judgmental statements, being ignored, crude talk?

A Successful Stress-Releasing Program

In the spring of 1978, during the last few months of my graduate work in education, I started looking for a job. I began substitute teaching at a residential home's campus school for adolescents who were diagnosed as emotionally disturbed. I eventually was asked to take a full-time teaching position. The level of acting-out behavior is especially high in the classroom for teenagers who are emotionally disturbed. These students' poor self-image often causes their behaviors to be controlled by internal fears and anxieties.

While teaching at this school, I had begun an exercise practice of yoga and meditation that helped me to release tension as well as to remain focused. At some point, I decided to see what the effects of a stress-releasing program might have on decreasing the acting-out behavior of my students in the classroom. The exercise program, which I called "centering," consisted of various daily muscle relaxation, guided imagery, and breathing techniques. The centering program was based on the assumption that tension and relaxation are incompatible.

Activity Sheet 7.1   Dealing With Problems

Problem: Nagging Students

Some suggestions:

1. Ignore the students who nag and praise those who don't.
2. Establish an alternative way to communicate complaints (e.g., Suggestion Box).
3. _____

Problem: Negative Colleagues

Some suggestions:

1. Avoid negative people whenever possible and do not talk about them.
2. Associate with positive-minded colleagues whenever possible.
3. _____

Problem: Angry Parent

Some suggestions:

1. Ask the parent to write down their concerns and establish a date on which you will sincerely respond to each concern.
2. Call or send home a note to the parent when their child is caught doing the "right thing."
3. _____

Problem: Overwhelming Amount of Paperwork

Some suggestions:

1. Prioritize your paperwork and complete it on time.
2. Do not bring a lot of work home without committing to a set schedule.
3. _____

Problem: Unmotivated Students

Some suggestions:

1. Incorporate an activator and summarizer at the beginning and end of all your lessons.
2. Make the material as relevant and as meaningful as possible to the students' lives.
3. _____

Problem: Inappropriately Dressed Students

Some suggestions:

1. Handle dress code issues privately. If the student is not aware of the dress code violation, suggest that he or she wear something over the shirt or turn it inside out.
2. If the student is wearing inappropriate clothes to be defiant, send him or her to an administrator.
3. _____

Problem: Unexpected Fire Drills

Some suggestions:

1. Teach your students the procedures you want them to follow and rehearse them.
2. Expect the unexpected. Stay calm and focused while maintaining civility and cooperation.
3. _____

Problem: Stolen Goods

Some suggestions:

Prevention

1. Often stealing is an impulsive act. Discuss the value of self-control and respecting others' private property. Leave classroom locked.
2. Don't leave personal belongings in the open or on your desk. Be aware when you take money out of your purse. Students are always observing.
3. _____

Dealing With Problem

1. Offer a reward for the return of the missing goods. Have a "no questions asked" policy.
2. Explain that the item may have been picked up by mistake. Give a certain amount of time for the item to be returned before involving an administrator.
3. _____

Problem: Note Passing

Some suggestions:

1. Give the students a choice: either put notes away or you will take them.
2. Note passing seems to be a ritual for middle school–aged children, but it should not take place during work time. Offer an alternative time to write notes. Improve your monitoring skills and lesson plans so all students are fully engaged in their work.
3. _____

Problem: Misbehavior While Watching a Video

Some suggestions:

1. Set the stage for the viewing. Create a worksheet for students to complete as they are watching the video.
2. Stop the video at predetermined points for discussion and answering worksheet questions.
3. _____

I initially taught students a method for inducing relaxation called Jacobson's Progressive Relaxation (Jacobson, 1973). This technique involved them progressively tensing and relaxing different major muscle groups. Since a muscle relaxes more after you tense it, you can greatly relax your whole body by first tightening your muscles—such as making fists—and then slowly releasing the tension. However, I also incorporated the conscious use of breathing techniques that I learned through practicing yoga and witnessed greater results than by just using physical methods alone. One of my yoga instructors once told me, "Our body is controlled by our mind and our mind is controlled by our breath." This was my experience as well. We often tell a student who is upset to gain their composure by relaxing and consciously "counting to ten."

I developed a consecutive four-week experiment with baseline information on acting-out behaviors. The results were impressive. The participation in the morning centering class, five days a week, significantly decreased the acting-out behavior in the classes that followed. When participation in centering ceased, acting-out behavior (e.g., getting out of seat without permission, loud blurting out of answers, using inappropriate language, hitting other students as an act of aggression) and classroom tension noticeably increased. The use of centering techniques increased the students' ability to control their tension and stress. Since my experiment, there have been numerous studies linking these sorts of centering exercises and techniques to greater self-control and well-being. In my books, *Group Exercises for Enhancing Social Skills and Self-Esteem, Vols. 1 & 2* (Khalsa, 1996, 1998), I offer several stress-releasing exercises that can easily be incorporated into your classroom's daily schedule.

Developing Inner Control

> We can't always change circumstances that are happening around us, but we can learn to control how we respond.

I once read that the main cause of injury during a California earthquake was not the earthquake itself but injury resulting from actions caused by panic.

The following strategies can help you develop the inner control necessary to respond effectively when an "earthquake" disrupts your classroom and school.

1. *Build a strong nervous system.* Take a class in yoga, martial arts, Tai Chi, or any other practice which works on stretching muscles and building strong nerves.

2. *Consciously breathe.* Practice conscious breathing when you're not feeling stressed and then use the technique when the warning signals appear. One simple technique is taking a long deep inhalation and, as you do, mentally say "inhale." Then slowly exhale and mentally say "relax." Repeat the same process for several minutes.

3. *Exercise regularly.* The operative word is regularly. People who work all day with children need to have time to exercise. It's that simple. Any exercise that increases oxygen to the body and creates a sweat is beneficial for maintaining a healthy body and mind.

MAINTAINING A POSITIVE MENTAL ATTITUDE: 15 STEPS

Things aren't the way they are, but the way you are.

—Anonymous

If your mind-set tends to be negative, you are far more likely to suffer from the ill effects of stress than a colleague with a positive mental attitude. A teacher of discipline is a positive thinker and interprets student behaviors as interesting challenges, whereas a negative person will see the same behavior as stressful impediments. The positive-minded teacher will not suffer the ill effects of stress. A wise colleague once shared his thoughts on thinking: "Teachers who learn that feelings are just a by-product of our thinking have an enormous edge in the classroom. They realize that to change a bad feeling requires simply changing the way we are thinking. By practicing this way of teaching, I expend far less energy being irritated at my students and consequently have more energy left over for being productive."

None of us is ever going to be a positive thinker 100 percent of the time—or maybe not even close to it—when dealing with the problems inherent in our profession. There will always be those times when we will feel overwhelmed. However, we can make incremental, sometimes even drastic, improvements in the way we think and therefore relate to our students and the responsibilities of being a teacher of discipline. Indeed, we can always improve the quality of our lives as individuals and as professional educators. Fortunately, many teachers have successfully used a variety of thinking and behavioral routines to cultivate a positive mental attitude. Positive thinking becomes a habit and, like anything else, becomes easier with practice. The following suggestions can help you develop and maintain a positive mental attitude:

15 Steps

1. Empathize, don't criticize.

2. Have an attitude of gratitude for what you have.

3. Let your students and colleagues know how much you appreciate them.

4. Help a student and a colleague feel important every day.

5. Say something positive about a student who is having difficulty behaving.

6. Do not speak adversely of yourself or others.

7. Do not listen to negativity about others.

8. Dress in clothes that make you look your best.

9. Keep company with other positive-minded colleagues.

10. Focus on finding solutions to problems that arise (when possible).

11. Be busy steering the boat and you will have no time to rock it.

12. Have a Student of the Month bulletin board (regardless of grade).

13. Write down your daily successes and build on them.

14. Set goals that will improve your life.

15. Be tolerant of others' mistakes.

RELEASING STRESS

You know how hard you work when teaching a full day, five days a week, thirty days a month, ten or more months a year. As I explained, tension sometimes builds so it can even be difficult to unwind in the evening or on weekends. When asking a colleague how their vacation was, it's not unusual to receive the response, "Not long enough." Sure, a long vacation would be nice, but what can you do *now* to clear your mind and release the undesired stress that could easily lead to burnout? I am, and other teachers

Positive Thinking

are, practicing many ways to release stress and bring more moments of insight and joy into our work day.

These 30 simple but powerful suggestions are offered for the purpose of heightening your perspective, patience, and wisdom as a teacher of discipline. They can help you respond to your disruptive students and school community more gracefully and with more confidence and ease. Try practicing the following strategies and activities to release stress by adding one each day, week, or month to your daily routine.

30 Techniques

1. Don't be so hard on yourself. Give yourself a break!

2. Take a short walk around the school grounds or a find a quiet spot and practice deep-breathing exercises.

3. Drink a cool glass of spring water.

4. Ease tension by laughing: "If you don't have a sense of humor, it's not funny."

5. Avoid eating a lot of junk food. It's not worth it.

6. Eat a wholesome breakfast.

7. Listen to uplifting music. Play an instrument.

8. Refuse to take rude and disruptive behavior personally.

9. Ask yourself, "How important is this going to be five years from now?"

10. Take yourself out to a nice restaurant and movie.

11. Meditate daily.

12. Lead an afterschool club.

13. Tackle busy work: avoid having paperwork build up.

14. Deal with the problems that cause you stress. Don't procrastinate.

15. Be totally involved with your students *but* don't be attached to the outcome.

16. Ask for help.

17. Spend time with people you care about.

18. Be upbeat with everyone—you're always listening to yourself.

19. Read a good book—even if it takes months to finish.

20. Write a book.

21. Recognize that good manners and grace are always in style.

22. Soak in a hot tub.

23. Cherish your family.

24. Set up a retirement plan and contribute to it as best as you can.

25. Drive a fairly new and very reliable car (especially in inclement weather).

26. After you have done all you can do to improve a situation in school, forget about it.

27. Enjoy a back massage.

28. Host a small dinner party for your favorite colleagues.

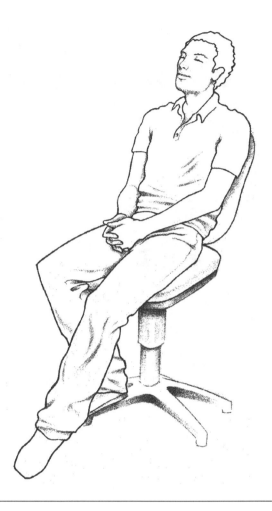

Serenity

29. Watch your favorite sporting event.

30. Never take yourself too seriously.

This following form can be given to your students to remind them of their attributes as a "whole student." It is surprising how much some students have lost touch with their selves, and you may find they have difficulty filling out this sheet. Guide them, teach them, and remind them of who each of them really is as a whole person. We want to recognize that our students are made up not just of intellect but also many more facets of their being. Howard Gardner's "Multiple Intelligences" theory (Gardner, 1993) reflects the whole child and the unique strengths they all possess. They should be constantly recognized for all their achievements.

Dealing with your behavior and how to act can get in the way with you really knowing YOU. I, _____, want to remind you that there's much more to you than your body and behavior. Your head, your heart, and your spirit, too, make up YOU.

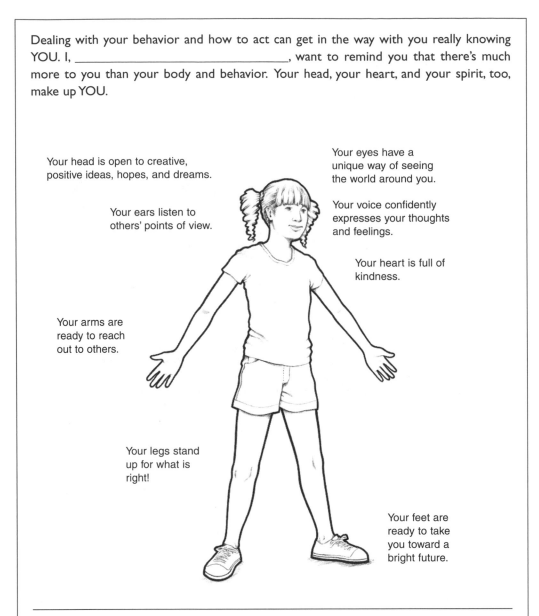

Your head is open to creative, positive ideas, hopes, and dreams.

Your eyes have a unique way of seeing the world around you.

Your ears listen to others' points of view.

Your voice confidently expresses your thoughts and feelings.

Your heart is full of kindness.

Your arms are ready to reach out to others.

Your legs stand up for what is right!

Your feet are ready to take you toward a bright future.

CONCLUDING THOUGHTS

Teaching discipline can be the most challenging as well as the most rewarding part of being a teacher. But, as I have stated, teaching discipline is a complicated kindness. It takes the right attitude to achieve success. If you conduct yourself in a manner that shows you are prepared for a confrontation, with certain students you will always be tested. So will the teacher who pretends there are no problems, who ignores unacceptable behavior and justifies it as self-expression. Teachers who conceive of themselves as primarily teaching a subject, instead of teaching students who happen to be studying those subjects, will also be unsuccessful in their approach to discipline.

Too many students are afraid of their teacher. They feel the teacher is an all-powerful person: "I must do what the teacher wants me to do, or else." When children have difficulty relating to their teacher, this will also affect their ability to behave and learn. Concentrate on the development of trust between you and your students. You want your students to say what they feel, even if it is as simple as "I didn't like my weekend. I had to visit my grandmother" or as complex as "I might not finish school because I'll never go to college." One quick way of building trust with your students is giving them as much control over their learning goals as possible. When we allow our students to have some control over their own learning, they often exceed our expectations.

I feel it's important to be human. I don't want students to see me as "the teacher" first and a person second. While maintaining professional boundaries, I want them to know who I am and understand why I became a teacher. I have found that if I share who I am, the things I like and dislike, it will encourage them to do the same. Then listening becomes paramount. We walk a tightrope where discipline is concerned, maintaining a delicate balance between rigidity and flexibility, blending nurturance, acceptance, and humor with realistic expectation, and natural and logical consequences. When the balance is found, then teaching can really begin.

Whether we accept it or not, we are role models for our students. Model an attitude of trust, high expectations, and confidence in their ability to achieve. Modeling a moment of discipline can mean more to a student than hours of discussion.

I've heard people say that if we can't help a child behave by the time they get to high school, we have lost them. Recently I helped coordinate a Black History Assembly for one of our middle schools. One of our guest speakers was a young African American man who, as he said, "was a son of the Springfield Public Schools." While growing up, he did not have a permanent home but lived in several foster care placements. In his clear, deep voice, he spoke of his past as a student with behavior problems. In the middle school he was placed in a self-contained classroom called the "pupil adjustment room." He was kicked out of two middle schools and, as he put it, "was saved by Mrs. Dailey." Mrs. Dailey was (and still is) the principal of his third middle school, Rebecca M. Johnson. She became his adviser and told him he had great potential but needed to start learning to control his behavior. Mrs. Dailey placed him in the mainstream classroom where he succeeded that year. His high school experience was a mixture of successes and failures. He dropped out after completing the eleventh grade. He then considered the military but ultimately heard the voices of his mentor teachers advising him to get an education, which he did. He presently is an educational coordinator and is completing his master's degree in administration. He wants to be a principal.

As teachers, parents, and caregivers, we must remember that we have one of the greatest privileges there is, the privilege of having an impact on the life of a developing child. It often takes one healthy adult role model to effect change in a child's life. My belief is that all students can learn. I give students opportunities to use their individual abilities, interests, and learning styles in their academic learning. This requires planning time— but it is time well spent making success available to all students regardless of the abilities of others in the classroom.

Finally, don't expect perfection from your students or from yourself. Look for progress and gradual change. Most students will distrust the teacher with the Messiah complex. Students with behavior and learning problems will respond positively to the reasonable demands of teachers who demonstrate common sense, firmness, and empathy. Students want their teachers to be successful in helping them to gain the skills necessary for them to become achievers. Teaching discipline takes disciplined effort. It is not easy, but it is truly worth the effort.

References

Banks, J., & McGee Banks, C. A. (Eds.). (1997). *Multicultural education: Issues and perspectives.* Boston: Allyn and Bacon.

Bloom, B. S. (1976). *Human characteristics and school learning.* New York: McGraw-Hill.

Brophy, J. E. (1996). *Teaching problem students.* New York: Guilford.

Caine, R. N., & Caine, G. (1994). *Making connections: Teaching and the human brain.* Menlo Park, CA: Addison-Wesley.

Canter, L., & Canter, M. (1976). *Assertive discipline.* Santa Monica, CA: Canter and Associates.

Carnes, J. (1998). *Teaching tolerance.* Montgomery, AL: Southern Poverty Law Center.

COMPASS Consulting (2005). 26 Sunnyside Street, Jamaica Plains, MA 02130.

Crawford, L., & Wood, C. (1999). *The responsive classroom.* Greenfield, MA: Northeast Foundation for Children.

Davis and Jordan (1994). *The academic cost of discipline: The relationship between suspension and expulsion and school achievement.* Bloomington, IN: Center for Evaluation and Education Policy, Indiana University.

DuPaul, G. & Stoner, G. (1994). *ADHD in the schools: Assessment and intervention strategies.* New York: Guilford Press.

Franklin, M. E. (1992). Culturally sensitive instruction practices for African American learners with disabilities. *Exceptional Children, 59,* 111–122.

Frederick, D. (n.d). *Indiana clearinghouse for citizenship and character education: Definitions.* http://reading.indiana.edu/chared/definitions.html

Gardner, H. (1993). *Multiple intelligences: The theory in practice.* New York: Basic Books.

Garibaldi, A. M. (1992). Educating and motivating African males to succeed. *Journal of Negro Education, 61*(1), 12–18.

Ginott, H. G. (1970). *Between teacher and child.* New York: Avon Books.

Gilbert, S. E., & Gay, G. (1985). Improving success in school of poor black children. *Phi Delta Kappan, 67,* 133–137.

Glasser, W. (1990). *The quality school: Managing students without coercion.* New York: Harper and Row.

Glasser, W. (1998). *Choice theory.* New York: Harper Collins.

Gordon, T. (1974). *T.E.T.: Teacher effectiveness training.* New York: Wyden Books.

Hallowell, E., & Ratey, J. (1994). *Driven to distraction.* New York: Pantheon Books.

Jacobson, J. E. (1973). *Teaching and learning new methods for old arts.* Chicago: National Foundation for Progressive Relaxation.

Kaufman, G., Raphael, L., & Espeland, P. (1999). *Stick up for yourself! Every kid's guide to personal power and self-esteem.* Minneapolis, MN: Free Spirit Publishers.

Kounin, J. (1970). *Discipline and classroom management.* New York: Holt, Rinehart, and Winston.

Khalsa, S. (1996 & 1998). *Group exercises for enhancing social skills and self-esteem* (Vols. 1 & 2). Sarasota, FL: Professional Resource Press.

Khalsa, S. (1999 & 2005). *The inclusive classroom: A practical guide for educators.* Tuscon, AZ: Good Year Books.

Khalsa, S. (2004). *Differentiated instruction: How to reach and teach all students.* Jacksonville, FL: Teaching Point Publishers.

Khalsa, D., & O'Keeffe, D. (2002). *The Kundalini yoga experience: Bringing body, mind and spirit together.* New York: Simon & Schuster.

Lieber, C. M., Lantieri, L., & Roderick, T. (1998). *Conflict resolution in high school: 36 lessons.* Cambridge, MA: Educators for Social Responsibility.

O'Neil, J. (2004, January). Real zingers: Tackling everyday discipline problems that make your classroom crazy. *NEA Today,* 24.

Olweus, D. (n.d.). *Bully intervention strategies that work.* http://www.education world.com

Owens, D. (1993). *Bully at school: What we know and what we can do.* Williston, VT: Blackwell Publishers.

Payne, R. (1996). Working with students from poverty: Discipline. *Instructional Leader, IX*(2), n.p. http://homepages.wmich.edu/~ljohnson/Payne.pdf

Payne, R. K. (2005). *A framework for understanding poverty.* Highlands, TX: Aha! Process.

Perls, F. (1983). *Gestalt therapy.* Hammond, IN: Owls Books.

Perry, T. (1993). *How racial and ethnic family and community characteristics affect children's achievement.* Research and Development Report No. 3 (pp. 1–3). Baltimore, MD: Center on Families, Communities, Schools & Children's Learning.

Robbins, A. (1994). *Giant steps: Small changes to make big a difference.* New York: Simon & Schuster.

Saphier, J., & Gower, R. (1990). *The skillful teacher: Building your teaching skills.* Carlisle, MA: Research for Better Teaching.

Simmons, R. (2003). *Odd girl out: The hidden culture of aggression in girls.* Fort Washington, PA: Harvest Books.

Townsend, B. (2000). The disproportionate discipline of African American learners: Reducing school suspensions and expulsions. *Exceptional Children,* 66(3), 381–391.

U.S. Commerce Department Census Bureau. (1997). *School retention rates.* Washington, DC: U.S. Commerce Department.

Walker, H. M. (1979). *The acting-out child: Coping with classroom disruptions.* Boston: Allyn and Bacon.

Wiggins, G., and McTighe, J. (1998). *Understanding by design.* Alexandria, VA: Association for Supervisin and Curriculum Development.

Wong, H. K., & Wong, R. T. (1998). *How to be an effective teacher: The first days of school.* Mountain View, CA: Harry K. Wong Publications.

Index

CORWIN PRESS

The Corwin Press logo—a raven striding across an open book—represents the union of courage and learning. Corwin Press is committed to improving education for all learners by publishing books and other professional development resources for those serving the field of PreK–12 education. By providing practical, hands-on materials, Corwin Press continues to carry out the promise of its motto: **"Helping Educators Do Their Work Better."**